W9-CGP-217

DISCOVERING
OUR HERITAGE

AUSTRALIA

A LUCKY LAND

BY AL STARK

DILLON PRESS
PARSIPPANY, NEW JERSEY

Photo Credits

(Photo credits from previous edition.)

Photographs have been reproduced through the courtesy of Al Stark and the *Detroit News*, and Milt and Joan Mann of Cameramann International Ltd. (©1987, pages 8, 19, 98–99, 102, 110).

(Second edition photo credits)

Front Cover: Map, Ortelius Design. *l.* Al Stark. *m.* Photo Researchers, Inc./© Brian Brake. *r.* Tom Stack & Associates/© Dave Watts.

Allsport Photography: 133. AP/Wide World Photos/Rick Rycroft: 13. Auscape International/Hans & Judy Beste: 82; © Jean-Paul Ferrero: 66; © Michael Jensen: 87; © J. M. La Roque: 18. Cameramann International, Ltd.: 117. Liaison International/ Russ Einhorn: 148. Photo Researchers, Inc./© Bill Bachman: 135; © Joyce Photographics: 79; © Mitch Reardon: 76. SBG: 5. Tom Stack & Associates/© Dave Watts: 71. Tony Stone Images/Robin Smith: 59. Courtesy, Yothu Yindi: 144. Map, Ortelius Design: 6.

Every effort has been made to locate the original sources. If any errors or omissions have occurred, corrections will be made.

Library of Congress Cataloging-in-Publication Data

Stark, Al
    Australia : a lucky land / by Al Stark.
      p. cm.—(Discovering our heritage)
    Includes bibliographical references and index.
    Summary: Describes the people, culture, geography, history, and customs of the "land down under."
    ISBN 0-382-39485-2
    1. Australia–Juvenile literature.   [1. Australia.]   I. Title
  II. Series
  DU96.S73   1997
  994—dc20   96-18445

Published by Dillon Press
A Division of Simon & Schuster
299 Jefferson Road, Parsippany, NJ 07054

Second Edition
Printed in the United States of America
10 9 8 7 6 5 4 3 2 1

CONTENTS

FAST FACTS ABOUT AUSTRALIA

Official Name: Commonwealth of Australia.

Capital: Canberra.

Location: Southeast of mainland Asia. The island of Australia lies between the Indian Ocean to the south and west and the South Pacific Ocean to the east.

Area: 2,978,147 square miles (7,713,364 square kilometers). *Greatest Distances:* north-south—1,950 miles (3,138 kilometers); east-west—2,475 miles (3,983 kilometers). *Coastlines:* 17,366 miles (27,948 kilometers), including 779 miles (1,254 kilometers) for Tasmania and 510 miles (821 kilometers) for offshore islands.

Elevation: *Highest*—Mount Kosciusko, 7,310 feet (2,228 meters) above sea level. *Lowest*—Lake Eyre, 52 feet (16 meters) below sea level.

Population: More than 18 million by 1995 estimate. *Distribution*—85 percent urban, 15 percent rural. *Density*—6 persons per square mile (2 persons per square kilometer).

Form of Government: Constitutional monarchy. Queen Elizabeth II of the United Kingdom is the head of state, and a prime minister is the head of the government.

Important Products: *Agriculture*—sheep, wool, cattle, dairy products, wheat, sugar cane, fruits, barley. *Manufacturing*—processed foods; iron, steel, and other metals; transportation equipment; paper; household

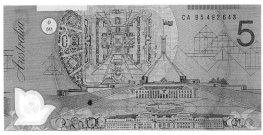

appliances. *Mining*—bauxite, coal, copper, gold, iron ore, lead, manganese, natural gas, nickel, opals, petroleum, silver, tin, tungsten, uranium, zinc.

Basic Unit of Money: Australian dollar.

Official Language: English.

Major Religions: Anglican; Roman Catholic.

Flag: Australia's flag has a dark blue background. In the upper left corner is a red-and-white British Union Jack. Below is a large white star for the Commonwealth. To the right are five white stars for the constellation Southern Cross.

National Anthems: *Advance Australia Fair* (national); *God Save the Queen* (royal).

Major Holidays: New Year's Day—January 1; Australia Day—January 26; Good Friday; Easter Sunday, Easter Monday (dates vary); ANZAC Day (Australian and New Zealand Army Corps Day)—April 25; Commonwealth Day—May 24; Christmas Day—December 25; Boxing Day—December 26.

THE LAND DOWN UNDER

"G'day, mate!"

This is the famous greeting of Australia, and all by itself it says a lot about the land and the people Down Under. The greeting is informal and friendly, and Australia is both of these.

Mate does not mean a sailor or one's spouse. It means "my special friend," and it is a very important word among Australians. In the harsh, forbidding interior of Australia in the early days it was very important to have a companion on whom one could rely. Life depended on it. People worked together or all suffered.

In Australia, these good friends who will stand by each other no matter what are called mates. Even in the modern and sophisticated Australia of the 1990s, "mateship" is very important.

So when people say to us, "G'day, mate," it means they expect we will be friends. They are willing to accept us as we are if we will accept them in the same way. This is exactly the manner in which Australians make visitors and travelers welcome, and it helps explain why Australians have so many friends around the world. Most Australians are lively and open people who enjoy life and good times, and they are very easy to like. Australians

An Australian "cowboy" checks the cattle at a water hole in Silver Pines in the Outback.

look around them and they like what they see. They call Australia the Lucky Country, and they mean it.

The Island Itself

Australia, the only continent that is also an island, lies well south of the equator at the far western edge of the Pacific Ocean. Its eastern coasts are washed by the South Pacific Ocean, and its western and southern coasts by the Indian Ocean. Australia got the nickname Down Under in the days when many homes and every classroom had a globe. Since the continent was down at the bottom of the globe, American and British people, located up toward the top, began to refer to Australia as Down Under. The island is about 2,000 miles (3,200 kilometers) southwest of Los Angeles. By airplane it takes about 13 hours to get from southern California to Australia.

Australia is an enormous country, covering almost 3 million square miles (almost 8 million square kilometers) in all. This makes it just a little bit smaller than the United States. Yet, whereas the population of the United States is more than 260 million, Australia's is just over 18 million. Australia is the least-populated continent in the world.

The British Link

Because Australia was settled by the British, English is the official language of the country. Another of Australia's links with England is religion. But religion for most Australians varies in the role it plays in day-to-day life. Formally, 36 percent of the population is Anglican. They are members of the Church of England, which is the official state church of England. Other Protestant groups make up about 25 percent of the population, and 33 percent is Roman Catholic. The Australian Constitution forbids a state religion and guarantees religious freedom. Because of this, most of the world's religions are represented in Australia.

Australia is the only continent that is all under one government, and it is formally known as the Commonwealth of Australia. Once ruled as a British colony, Australia is still tied to the United Kingdom. The United Kingdom's monarch, Queen Elizabeth II, is also queen of Australia and its official head of state, but she has very little power in the Australian government. Her main purpose is to serve as a symbol of the historic tie between the two countries.

Officially, the federal government of Australia is headed by a governor general, who represents the queen. But, like the queen, the governor general has a role in Australia that is mainly symbolic.

Australia has a parliamentary system of government and a prime minister to run its day-to-day affairs. The Federal Parliament is the main governing body. Like the United States Congress, it has an upper house called the Senate and a lower house called the House of Representatives. Bills become law after they are passed by both houses of Parliament. The prime minister is the leader of the political party or the coalition (combination) of parties with the majority of seats in the House of Representatives.

On the present-day political scene, three political parties are dominant—the Australian Labor party, the Liberal party, and the National party, which represents farmers and rural Australians.

Australia's Liberal party and its Labor party have both had their turns in office. The Liberal party is actually the more conservative party, and the Labor party is made up of liberals with a strong labor backing. Since World War II, Australia's government has been most often conservative. John Howard was elected prime minister in 1996. He headed a Liberal party–National Party coalition.

Australian States

Australia has six states. The five on the mainland are New South Wales, Victoria, South Australia, Western

John Howard waves to the crowd after his victory in the 1996 general election. He replaced Labor party leader Paul Keating.

Australia, and Queensland. The sixth state is the island of Tasmania, off the southern coast. The Northern Territory has the special status of a self-governing territory. The federal government administers the Australian Capital Territory (similar to the District of Columbia in the United States), where the capital, Canberra, is located.

The states and the Northern Territory each have their own regional government and measure of independence. However, because almost all authority to tax in Australia is reserved for the federal government, the states aren't as independent as they like to say they are.

Each state has its own capital, which functions not only as the state's political center but as its commercial, industrial, and cultural center as well. Sydney, a wonderfully lively city, is the capital of New South Wales and is Australia's largest city. Melbourne, state capital of Victoria, is elegant and dignified. Melbourne hosted the 1956 Olympics. Adelaide, a lovely, quiet city, is capital of South Australia. Perth, host for the America's Cup sailing races for four years, is the capital of Western Australia. In the Northern Territory, Darwin is the capital and in Queensland, it is Brisbane. Tasmania's capital is Hobart.

Each of these cities is located near a natural harbor on the seacoast. The coastal strip on the southern and eastern edges of Australia has been called one of the nicest locations in all the world to live. It is cooled by the sea breeze in the summer, and the winters are mild. The rain keeps vegetation green throughout the year. This temperate strip runs from above Brisbane on the eastern coast of Australia around to Adelaide on the southern coast. Almost three fourths of Australia's population lives in this area.

The Great Empty

The rest of Australia is sparsely populated because most of the country's interior is desert or near-desert. Australia is the driest continent on earth. The government acknowledges that much of the interior is unlivable, and travelers can discover that for themselves. It is possible to drive all day long in the dry interior deserts of Australia and see no living creatures except for sheep and kangaroos.

Australia is also the flattest continent, though it does have some mountain ranges. In the southeastern corner of the country are the Australian Alps, which consist of several ranges. The Snowy Mountains are the best-known of these, and Australia's highest peak, Mount Kosciusko, is located here. In the winter, many of the Snowy Mountains' peaks are covered with snow, which makes the area popular among skiers.

In central Australia rise the Macdonnell and Musgrave ranges, but these are much lower in elevation than the Australian Alps. South of the Macdonnell Ranges is Ayers

*Skiers enjoy the snowfields at Smigging Holes on
Mount Kosciusko in New South Wales.*

Rock. Every year, hundreds of tourists journey into the desert to see this giant stone hill. Ayers Rock is about 1,000 feet (300 meters) high and over 1.5 miles (2.4 kilometers) long! Except for these few mountain ranges, much of Australia, especially its interior, resembles a tabletop.

The interior of Australia is known as the Outback, famous the world over as one of the great rugged frontiers. The interior is also home to one of the most fascinating ethnic peoples anywhere, the Australian Aborigines. For thousands of years, these tribes lived in the harsh desert, struggling for survival. The ancestors of today's Aborigines were the first people to inhabit the land of Australia. Since the arrival of white settlers, their history has been similar to that of American Indians in the United States.

Australians, who have a rich way with slang, have other names besides the Outback for their strange, hard, and unfriendly middle country. Some simply call it Beyond. Others call it Beyond Beyond. Four great deserts—the Simpson Desert, the Great Sandy Desert, the Gibson Desert, and the Great Victoria Desert—come together in the almost exact geographic center of Australia. This area is commonly known as the Red Center because the rocks and sand are reddish in color. Some Australians simply refer to everything any distance from the coast as the Great Empty and let the name-calling go at that.

The red sands of the Simpson Desert show why the Australian desert is called the Red Center.

As you travel inland from the sea, no matter where on the coast you start, you will pass through miles and miles of scrubland. Here the grass is sparse and the trees low and weak-looking. After this scrubland comes the desert, the really empty part of Australia. If you look at a map of the Outback, you might be surprised to see that rivers run through it and that the region is dotted with lakes. But these are almost always dry, sometimes for years at a time. There is one Outback lake called Lake Disappointment, and its name tells its story.

Ayers Rock, in the heart of the Red Center of Australia, is probably the nation's best-known natural tourist attraction.

Because Australia is in the Southern Hemisphere, winter occurs in July and August, the reverse of what occurs in North America and Europe. Spring rains come in September and October. Sometimes the rain comes in torrents, and the Outback's dry rivers and lakes flood quickly. Sometimes the rain is only a few drops that kick up dust.

In the Australian summer, November to February, temperatures in the Outback quite commonly reach 130 to 140 degrees Fahrenheit (54 to 60 degrees Celsius). In this terrible heat everything shimmers and seems to constantly change shape. The few trees in the deep Outback have had to struggle in their parched climate to survive. Their branches tend to be twisted and bent, as if the fight has deformed them.

Australia's Gold

As strangely empty as it is, the Outback is the source of much of Australia's wealth. The land gave up gold to the people brave and strong enough to explore it in the early days. Today mines still produce gold in large quantities. In a couple of places, the Outback is rich in opals, those milky jewels carrying streaks of fire. Nearly all of the world's top-quality opals come from Australia, from diggings near tiny towns such as Lightning Ridge in New South Wales and Coober Pedy in South Australia.

There are also important diamond and silver mines in the Outback, as well as considerable reserves of less glamorous resources such as copper, iron ore, lead, manganese, nickel, tin, and zinc. Australia is a major supplier of coal to countries like Japan and leads the world in the production of bauxite, the ore from which aluminum is made. There are large deposits of uranium, a radioactive element used in nuclear weapons and fuel, especially in the Northern Territory. For political reasons, much of the uranium is not mined.

Along with mining, farming is a very important element in Australia's economy. Farmers in Western Australia, particularly, grow immense crops of wheat that they market around the world. Queensland also produces wheat in large quantities. In the parts of the state where the climate is almost tropical (the northern coastal area around Cairns) grow vast quantities of sugar cane, which is also exported.

All over the Outback, except in the driest deserts, roam sheep. Wool from the merino sheep gave the country its first real economy, and Australia still produces 35 percent of the world's wool. Australia has about eight sheep for every person. Most people think of the kangaroo or the cuddly koala when they think of Australia, but actually the sheep is by far the most important animal in Australia's history.

These merino rams (male sheep) are herded together at a stud ranch in Western Australia.

Another industry, relatively new to Australia, is wine producing. Growers have found many sites suitable for growing grapes, and Australian wines are now appearing around the world. A wine called the 1990 Penfolds Grange was named wine of the year for 1995 by *Wine Spectator* magazine, the first time a wine from a place other than France or California had won the prize. Seven other Australian wines made the Top 100 list.

Coastal Cities

The wealth of the Outback flows through the cities on the coast. Sydney, located in the southeastern part of the country on what is perhaps the most beautiful harbor in the world, is Australia's main center of business, finance, and the arts. Metropolitan Sydney spreads north and south along the Pacific Ocean coast and inland about 50 miles (80 kilometers) to the Blue Mountains, a natural barrier.

Nearly a sixth of all Australians live in greater Sydney. Its population totals more than 3 million and is still growing. Sydney is home to one of the wonders of the twentieth century, the magnificent seashell-shaped building that is the Sydney Opera House (see pages 87, 99, 98–99). The inhabitants of Sydney come from almost every part of the world, and the variety of people gives the city great energy.

Melbourne, south and west of Sydney, is a little more conservative. It is a city of old wealth and commerce, more stately than the bubbly Sydney. The second largest city, Melbourne is home to just under 3 million residents.

Adelaide, from which some of the important explorations were launched in the early days, has about 1 million inhabitants. It may be the prettiest Australian city of them all. Close to the sea, it is bordered on one side by the Adelaide Hills, where many people live up above the city proper. Adelaide's city center is surrounded by a broad greenbelt of parks, playing fields, and nature trails. This greenbelt gives it a calm, restful atmosphere.

The Murray River, Australia's longest permanently flowing river, empties into the ocean southeast of Adelaide. The Murray starts in the Snowy Mountains and winds westward about 1,600 miles (2,576 kilometers) before reaching the sea. Along the way, it is fed by the country's longest river, the Darling. The Darling River begins in central New South Wales and flows southwestward about 1,700 miles (2,737 kilometers) before joining the Murray. The Darling is dry in the winter. For most of the river's length, however, its flow is greater in the summer because of increased rainfall in its area. Thus, when most of the other southern rivers dry up, the Darling still supplies water to the Murray.

Perth is on the Indian Ocean, far to the west of Sydney and the other large cities. Yet, ever since a yacht from the Royal Perth Yacht Club stunned the world by winning the America's Cup from the United States in 1983, Perth has felt directly at the center of things Australian. An enormous amount of attention has been focused on Perth since that yacht race, and hundreds of millions of dollars' worth of new construction has taken place there. The city is booming, and the 1 million people who live there are proud of its progress.

Australia is famous for its stretches of beautiful coastline. This is a crowded city beach in Newcastle in New South Wales.

Darwin, capital of the Northern Territory, is far removed from everywhere else on the other side of the vast Outback. Only about 65,000 people live there. It is the part of Australia closest to Asia, and it has sizable communities of people from Indonesia and other parts of Asia. Darwin is well within the steamy tropics. To combat the heat, there are fans on the ceilings of hotel rooms and the men wear walking shorts rather than trousers.

Brisbane, halfway up the eastern coast, has a population of about 1,200,000. It is a country town that has grown and grown but has never lost its small-town feel. Its tropical climate makes Queensland a favorite winter vacation place for Australians, much as Florida is the warm-weather getaway for many Americans in the winter season.

Hobart, on the island state of Tasmania, is a city of just under 200,000 people. Tasmania is a rugged place. Because it is the part of Australia closest to Antarctica, it is just about the only place in the country where a person can expect it to be really cold in the winter.

The federal government is located at Canberra, the only major Australian city not on a seacoast. Both Sydney and Melbourne wanted to be the site of the federal capital, and a political disagreement developed. The solution finally reached in 1913 was to locate the capital halfway between the two rival cities, creating a new city. It was named Canberra. This Aboriginal word means "meeting place." The capital is part of neither state; instead it is part of the Australian Capital Territory. Canberra has about 250,000 residents, many of them government employees. The city plans were drawn by an American architect, Walter Burley Griffin, and so Canberra's general design resembles that of the District of Columbia in the United States.

Beaches and the Great Barrier Reef

Australia is blessed with endless beaches, wide and sandy, and every state boasts about its shoreline. Queensland not only has beautiful beaches; it also has the one great natural wonder in Australia, the Great Barrier Reef. The Great Barrier Reef hugs the Pacific coast of the continent and runs from Bundaberg, just north of Brisbane, all the way to New Guinea, a distance of 1,200 miles (1,932 kilometers).

The reef is a living thing, made up of layers and layers of coral polyps, which are tiny shelled sea animals. The brightly colored reef is home to 300 varieties of coral, from blue to shades of pink and purple. There are, by best count, 1,400 varieties of fish living around the reef, and they are as colorful as the coral. In season great gamefish, notably marlin, gather off the reef, and anglers come from all over

In this aerial view of the Great Barrier Reef, parts of the long reef chain rise up through the clear blue water.

the world to fish for them. Other vacationers enjoy the reef as well, and there are many island resorts nearby to host them. Travelers dive at the reef, walk it in low tide, and fly over it in special aircraft. In 1979, Australia created the Great Barrier Reef Marine Park, with its research center and bird sanctuary.

More and more Americans are going Down Under on vacation to see Australia for themselves, and many American firms are represented there, too. Qantas Airways Limited, Australia's only international airline, connects the continent with all the world. Many Australians have traveled to the United States and Europe, where they have distinguished themselves against all competition in the arts, popular entertainment, science, and sports.

Australia has opened its doors not only to travelers but also to immigrants from much of the world. Today, Australia has a richly diverse population made up of many nationalities. A number of European countries other than England have helped populate Australia, including Ireland, Italy, Greece, the former Yugoslavia, Germany, and the Netherlands. In addition, Australia has made itself something of a haven for people from the troubled spots of the world. Since World War II it has taken in many people from Eastern Europe. Lately it has become the new home of people from the war-torn areas of the Middle East and Southeast Asia.

Though this friendly country welcomes thousands each year, it sometimes seems to ignore the problems of its own people. More and more Australian children fail to complete their education, and many face an uncertain future. Australia also wrestles with the situation of the Aborigines, never quite understanding the difficulties that its native Australians face. This situation is disturbing, because many Aborigines live in poverty on the fringes of Australian society.

Although Australia enjoys a generally high standard of living, the government now spends one quarter of its national budget on welfare aid for the poor. Some of Australia's leaders worry about the economy and question whether it will continue to support the comfortable lifestyle of most people.

But for the most part, there is little worry evident among the people of Australia. Relaxed and friendly, they are confident about their future.

THE COLORFUL AUSSIES

The Aussie character is difficult to pinpoint because of the great variety in Australia's people. The culture has become a blend of a strong British heritage, the huge number of immigrants that flooded the continent after World War II, and the Australian Aborigines.

But if one thing distinguishes the Australian character and personality, it is the Aussie's streak of independence. Australians prize their individual freedoms, and they believe that one person's opinions are as important as another's, even when one is a bishop and the other is a baker. Although they elect leaders, they are distrustful of authority if it is too heavy-handed. Given a choice, Australians tend to side with the little man or woman—the underdog.

These national traits could date back to the early days of the country's settlement. Most of the first white Australians were convicts from England, some convicted with good reason and some imprisoned unfairly. For many of them, being transported to Australia provided a new chance at life, and they were determined never to be locked up or hemmed in again. Those who had been jailed without just cause found it hard to trust authority ever again, wherever they found themselves.

*An Outback sheep rancher north of New South Wales
adjusts some feed pails.*

Another factor in the development of the Australian character was Australia itself. In this vast, new country, those who wanted room where they could live with no bosses but themselves could find it. It is no surprise that the Outback, that immense, empty space, has had such a great influence on the Australian personality. Australians admire the men and women who pushed into the interior—the swagmen, the sheep ranchers, and even the lawbreaking bushrangers—and have inherited many character traits and attitudes from them.

Slang, Australia-Style

Australians have a gift for the sarcastic remark, particularly when they think people are making too much of themselves. Often the tart remarks are delivered in a rich and earthy slang, famous the world over.

This colorful language is spoken with the Aussie version of an English accent that has a flavor all its own. In Australia, *day* sounds like "die," and *prime minister* sounds like "prymista." Some think the slang was started by ex-convicts who purposely mangled proper English as a way of thumbing their noses at an England that had the nerve to put them in prison. There is no limit to what Australians can do with slang. For instance, *have a Captain Cook* means "have a look." A policeman is a *walloper*, and a busybody is a *stickybeak*. A *silvertail* is someone who thinks he or she is better than anyone else. Australian slang is easy once you get the swing of it, and it is fun.

The Wandering Swagmen

Of all the Australians who have been celebrated in story and song, none is more famous than the swagman. He carried his belongings in a roll on his back. That was his swag. From this roll or from his belt hung a tin cup, which he used as a pot to boil water for his tea. He would tie small corks to the brim of his hat like a fringe. When the flies and gnats that swarm through the Outback got too thick about his face, he would simply give his head an energetic shake and the corks would dance, shooing the flies away.

Particularly in the early days when there were no vehicles, swagmen walked wherever they went, sometimes for tremendous distances, even from one coast to another. They slept outside most of the time, and they ate whatever they could fish out of water holes or hunt down along the way.

Many of them had no real home. They lived wherever they were. Although they might pair up if they met someone they didn't mind traveling with, each was on his own and each followed his own direction. Some used only first names. Some used nicknames and never told anyone who they really were.

Some swagmen were never anything but tramps who thieved what they could. They had been pickpockets and cutpurses in England, and they never changed their ways. The well-known song "Waltzing Matilda" tells the story of a swagman who drowns trying to get away with a sheep he has stolen.

But many of the swagmen were skilled at some trade or at least handy. Among these were men who had never been real criminals but who had been imprisoned in

England because they owed debts they could not pay. When they went into the Outback, they were able to find work whenever they wanted it. The sheep ranchers could always use another hand, particularly one who might be able to repair equipment or work with animals. As settlement spread inland, common trails developed. These usually led from one isolated sheep station to another— through tiny Outback towns, past water holes, and past scrub forests where game might be found. The feet of the swagmen helped smooth out these trails, which became Australia's first rough roads.

A swagman might make his way across the entire country on these trails, stopping at a ranch or farm to work a few months and then moving on to the next one. Even if there was no work for him, he was welcome to stay for a meal and sleep in the bunkhouse.

A common code grew up in the Outback. No traveler was refused food or shelter. The Outback was hard and dangerous. Everyone helped everyone else because people understood that their own lives might one day depend on the assistance of another. When the settlers finally built towns in the Outback, it became a rule at the hotels that anyone who walked into town ate and drank free. Anyone who rode in or arrived in a vehicle had to pay—and pay a very steep price.

Tony Mortress is the modern version of Australia's famous Outback wanderer. Now a ranger in Kakadu National Park, he has moved around the country from job to job. He has been a guide, miner, and camp assistant since he left high school.

Above all, the swagmen were free and beholden to no one, wandering wherever they wished, wherever their feet led them. Australia's enormous open spaces gave them plenty of room, and they took advantage of it.

There is still a lot of room to roam in Australia, and the spirit of the swagman is still alive. Even in today's Australia it is not at all uncommon to meet carpenters or bricklayers who have worked in every state of the country, just moving around as the whim strikes them. Nor is it unusual to find a park ranger who, since finishing high school, has been a gold miner, a sheepherder, a camp guide, and an opal miner, just for the enjoyment of trying new things and seeing new places.

Gold and the Bushrangers

The Outback always meant hard work. In 1851, gold was discovered near Bathurst on the Macquarie River, about 200 miles (about 300 kilometers) west of Sydney. For the people who rushed to the gold fields, hard work began to mean a chance for a big payoff or maybe even a fortune. That possibility also attracted robbers, who in the early days of Australia were called bushrangers.

The most famous bushranger of all was Ned Kelly, who was born during the early 1850s in northern Victoria to Irish immigrant parents. Kelly, by all the evidence, was nothing but a thief and a killer, but he benefited from Australia's great affection for the underdog in any argument against authority.

Gold meant wealth. Wealth often meant big business and big banks. It was almost guaranteed that anyone who picked the pockets of the wealthy by robbing their gold wagons would become something of a hero to the working classes, whose lives were often made up of endless dull labor and who didn't like the upper classes much anyway. Kelly was a clever outlaw who sometimes took whole towns hostage. He portrayed himself as a Robin Hood, and he had many fans. Songs were written about him, and they are still sung. But he overreached himself finally and was captured and hanged when he was just 26 years old.

The Working People

Today, Australians still believe in equality. Class is not defined by wealth. Most Australians consider themselves to be members of the middle class, which holds the same general values of middle classes everywhere. It prizes good conduct, order, and public safety. The middle class pays taxes to provide modern police forces, and it likes to see its police on the job. But every once in a while a police department in modern Australia will complain that it is not getting cooperation from the public. When that happens, someone always remarks that this is a throwback to the attitudes of the earliest white Australians, who were suspicious of law enforcement officers and frequently sided with those the officers were after.

Traditionally, labor unions have been very strong in Australia. This also stems from the country's early days and the experiences of the swagmen. If they didn't like the work that they were asked to do on one sheep station, they'd quit and go to another. Station owners and foremen quickly learned to make sure that their hands agreed with the work scheduled for the day. This was a measure of self-protection. If a sheep station's workers marched off just at shearing time, a year's work might be lost as well as any profit.

Business owners from England who came to Australia in the 1800s were amazed when they listened to a ranch foreman or a mining boss consulting with workers about what should be done instead of ordering them to do this or that. This was long before the existence of industrial labor unions, and it was unheard of in the mills and on the farms of Europe. But it was already the Australian way.

Today there is ample evidence of the strength of modern labor unions and of Australia's continuing respect for the efforts of working people. Australians are protected in illness, unemployment, injury, and old age by a broad selection of government programs. Most working Australians get four weeks of vacation and many get six, all of it paid, and also a vacation bonus.

Every now and then some critic says that it is too easy for working people in Australia. These critics worry that if life is too easy, the country may fall behind other nations in a world where change follows change. But most Australians work just as hard as anyone else. It took effort, skill, and brains to build cities as splendid as Australia's. Making a living in the Outback took grinding, brave effort and determination. Everywhere you look in Australia, you see the rewards of hard work.

The Flood of Immigrants

A very rich influence on the national character and personality has come from abroad—from the great number

of immigrants who have been welcomed to Australia since
World War II ended in 1945. Roughly 4.75 million people
from 120 other countries have settled in Australia since
the war. England continues to contribute more new
Australians than any other country, and the rest of
Europe—particularly Greece and Italy—also contributes a
significant number. But people from Asia and Oceania, the
vast Pacific with all its islands, are also sending so many
people to Australia that in real ways they are changing the
look and flavor of the country.

Many new Australians have had to learn English, and
many have had to struggle to fit into the country's society.
But all in all their transformation into Australians has been
without particular conflict. They have enriched Australia
with their own cultures and viewpoints.

The Aborigines

The Aborigines lived in Australia long before the
white people came, but they have little influence on the
national character of the country as it is today. From the
time the first white settlers landed in the late eighteenth
century, Aborigines were pushed aside. In the 200 years
since, they have never gained a place in the Australian
mainstream.

Whites have a fascination with the Aborigines' ability
to survive in the worst parts of the interior. The Aborigines

*A pet possum sits on the head of a 14-year-old Aborigine girl
from the Tiwi tribe of Bathurst Island.*

are regarded as masters at tracking others in the wastelands of the Outback, and even today they are asked to help when a child, camper, or adventurer is lost in the wilderness. But they are only called when all else has failed.

Today there are about 267,000 Aborigines left in Australia, making up about 1.5 percent of the population. They are too few to have political power except as scars on Australia's conscience. The bush life no longer is appealing to young Aborigines who have seen cars and movies and have eaten at McDonald's. Yet far too many of them drop out of school, which means that few are able to hold better than low-paying jobs. Many young Aborigines are idle, and many get into trouble. The great majority of Aboriginal families live on welfare.

The many different kinds of people who now live in Australia have changed the once very British flavor of the country into a rich cultural blend. All the people of Australia seem to share a love of their land, its open spaces, its wonderful climate, and its sense of freedom.

THE BRITISH GO ASHORE

Before 1788, when the white settlers arrived, 300,000 to 350,000 Aborigines had all of Australia to themselves. Australia was practically empty. The Aborigines were immigrants themselves, in the best opinion of scholars. It is believed that they were originally Southeast Asian people who migrated by choice or were driven by force to what we know as Australia. They came by boat or traveled on foot over the land bridges that once connected Australia to New Guinea and Asia. When the seas rose, the land bridges disappeared under water, and Australia was left an island. No one knows who may have been living in Australia when the Aborigines arrived.

In Australia, it is estimated that there were about 500 separate tribes of Aborigines. The tribes were most commonly organized along family lines, and many tribes were quite small.

To the best of anyone's knowledge, a single Aboriginal nation never existed in Australia. Although tribes had contact with each other, sometimes friendly and sometimes hostile, each kept itself separate from the others. Some tribes lived in the deserts, others near the coasts. Each had its own traditional area, but all moved from place to place within their areas as the seasons changed. They built no permanent settlements or villages.

The most desirable locations for tribes to live were those along the few rivers in Australia that could be counted on to have water in them. Living was easier where there was a dependable water supply. More plants grew there, animals would come to the river, and fish swam in its water. When tribes fought each other, it was often over rights to the best-watered camping grounds along the rivers. Wherever they lived, Aborigines were hunters and gatherers. They didn't plant crops or raise animals for food.

The land was life to the Aborigines, and it was of the highest importance in their spiritual lives. Most believed in what they call the Dreaming, when the spirits shaped the world and gave it life. The spirits then went to live in a particular tree or a particular rock. These trees and rocks became sacred to the Aborigines, to be honored, preserved, and safeguarded. Ayers Rock is one of these sacred Aboriginal spots.

Although one tribe of Aborigines might have fought another over a particularly fertile and game-filled piece of land, most believed the earth did not belong to any one person but belonged to all. The berries on a bush belonged to the people who happened to come across them. No one's permission was needed to eat them. They were a gift from

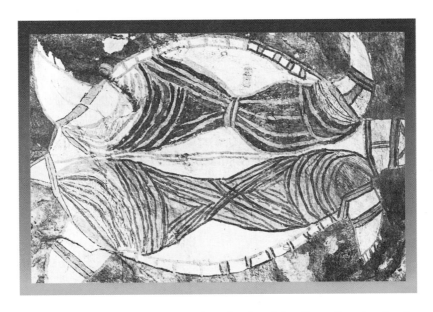

Aborigines hunted turtles on the islands of the Great Barrier Reef. They drew such pictures as this one on cave walls.

the earth. They felt the same way about game. Any animal or fish belonged to the person who could catch it.

Aborigines often painted elaborate designs of human and animal figures in caves or on rocks and bark. Some Aborigines carved figures from wood or stone and then painted them. Others wove beautiful baskets, mats, and bags. Today many Aboriginal paintings are collected, and wall paintings are protected by the law.

It is estimated that the Aborigines had Australia to themselves for 35,000 or 40,000 years. During this time they had no idea there was a place, now called Europe, where white people had learned to build sailing ships that could carry them across the seas to many strange and different places.

On the Map

Australia first appeared on maps drawn in Europe in about 1500. Early Chinese and Arab voyagers talked of a great southern land east of India, and their tales were carried back to Europe. The earliest maps only guessed at where Australia was and what it looked like. No one knew it was surrounded by water; people assumed it was attached to Antarctica.

Mapmakers named this mysterious place in Latin, calling it *Terra Australis Incognita*. *Terra* means "land"; *australis* means "southern"; and *incognita* means "unknown"—the Unknown Southern Land. The greatest exploring nations of Europe, in the first flush of their seagoing power, all hunted for Australia.

Some historians think the Portuguese were already familiar with Australia's eastern coast in the fifteenth century, although for reasons unknown they neither announced it nor tried to settle there. In 1606 a Portuguese, Luis Vaez de Torres, sailed along the southern coast of New Guinea, in the narrow strait that separates it from Australia's northern coast. Torres gave his name to the strait, but as far as anyone knows, he sailed through it without catching sight of Australia.

The Dutch did better. Willem Jansz, sailing from Java in Indonesia, landed on the western shore of the Cape York Peninsula, at the far northeastern tip of Australia. He is regarded as the first European known to have set foot on the continent. He decided the prospects for treasure or settlement were poor, and he found the natives unfriendly. He reported to his superiors that he found no good reason to stay or settle. Over the next 35 years other Dutch explorers came to the coast, mostly by accident, having been blown off course. None of them reported anything more encouraging than Jansz had. The Dutch decided this could not be the Unknown Southern Land that the Chinese and Arabs had talked of, and they continued to look elsewhere.

In 1642 the Dutch sent Abel Tasman out to look again. He found Tasmania, which he called Van Dieman's Land, and he also discovered New Zealand and the islands of Fiji. The Tasman Sea, which separates Australia and New Zealand, is named for him.

The first British sailor known to have landed in Australia was William Dampier, a part-time explorer and a part-time pirate. Dampier scouted the west coast and went ashore at King Sound in 1688. He was as discouraged as Jansz had been. He sailed off, firmly believing that it would be a waste of time to seek trade or gold there.

Australia lay undisturbed for almost another century. On April 28, 1770, Captain James Cook, on his way back to England after a long voyage, steered his ship into a natural harbor on the Pacific coast, just south of

Captain James Cook

present-day Sydney. Cook carried two famous botanists with him who went ashore and brought back to the ship many unusual specimens of animal, plant, and bird life. Seeing how excited the botanists were at their discoveries, Cook decided to name the bay where his ship was anchored Botany Bay.

Cook and his crew stayed in Australian waters until August, making their way up the entire coast as far as the tip of Cape York Peninsula. Before sailing for home, Cook claimed the eastern half of Australia for the king of

England. In London, he reported that although he had gone ashore at Botany Bay, he did not think this was the sought-after Terra Australis Incognita. He thought it was part of New Holland, the name given by Jansz and other Dutch explorers to the land when they first found and rejected it.

Cook set out again in 1772. After crisscrossing the vast Pacific as far as Antarctica, he proved once and for all that most of the ocean was empty. If there was a great southern land anywhere, it must have been the land he had seen.

A Prison Colony

Shortly, England would have great use for the land Cook had claimed. England was experiencing terrible social problems. Its cities, London being the worst case, were overrun by unemployed people. Slums grew and spread. Widespread crime added more trouble. To preserve order, the government enacted harsh laws under which people could be given long prison sentences for very minor crimes, even for being unable to pay debts. So many people were imprisoned that the jails overflowed, and people feared the spread of disease. Rotting ships that were tied up along the Thames River in London were turned into jails. They were crammed full of men, women, and children who had run afoul of the law. Conditions were horrible, and all Londoners were appalled and frightened.

The solution was to send prisoners to the far colonies. There they could work off their sentences as laborers in the new settlements, under the control of colonial governors and troops. This practice was known as "transportation." A criminal or a debtor was not sentenced to prison but was given transportation to one of the colonies. Under the terms of transportation, convicts could earn their freedom eventually, when they had worked off enough years to pay for the crime.

Authorities sent some convicts to America. But, by 1770 when Captain Cook sailed into Botany Bay, the American colonies were already displaying the restlessness and itch for freedom that would result in the United States' Declaration of Independence. No longer able to use America as a prison, or penal, colony, England's eye fell upon Australia. In May 1787, eleven ships under the command of Captain Arthur Phillip sailed from London for Australia carrying about 1,000 passengers, three fourths of them convicts.

Landing in Sydney

It took Captain Phillip's little fleet eight months to reach Botany Bay. He anchored there briefly and sent scouts up and down the coast. They reported a much more desirable and safer harbor just to the north, and so Phillip

The early settlers hoisted the British flag when the First Fleet landed at Sydney Harbor.

sailed there. This place is called Port Jackson or Sydney Harbor, and it was there, on January 26, 1788, that Phillip sent the first white Australians ashore.

Phillip's ships are known to Australians as the First Fleet. His landing at Sydney Harbor is celebrated every year as part of Australia Day ceremonies. Phillip named Sydney for Viscount Sydney, the secretary of the department of the English government that supervised colonial affairs. It was the first settlement in Australia. Sydney has always been the seat of government for New South Wales, Australia's first and most populous state.

The Aborigines

The Aborigines watched from the shore as Captain Phillip landed the first white settlers. No one asked the Aborigines' permission to come ashore; no one ever negotiated with them for land. They did not resist the landing. What they did, by all accounts, was watch the whites unload their ships and come ashore.

To the white settlers, the Aborigines were primitive savages. They had built no towns or cities. They knew nothing of Western civilization or its rules and manners. Many went about naked.

The few settlers who did take an interest in the Aborigines usually tried to convert them, clothe them, and teach them white ways. Some whites treated them as curiosities. Many more whites showed the Aborigines terrible cruelty. Aborigines were killed because they were regarded as thieves and sometimes just because they were regarded as a nuisance. The Aborigines did little to help their own cause. When they learned the whites had stores of food, some Aborigines stopped hunting and fishing, and begged because begging was easier work. Although some Aborigines fought the whites, they never teamed up to make an effective fighting force.

Whites took the best land. Because the Aborigines had never built anything on the land, whites assumed it was available to them. Although whites employed some

Aborigines as herders and trackers in the Outback, whites were always the bosses. The Aborigines were driven to the outskirts of Australian society.

The Early Pioneers

The early days of Australia's first settlement were very grim. The wheat seed that the settlers had brought from England spoiled during the journey and would not germinate when planted in Australia. Their sheep were taken by Aborigines or stolen by convicts up to their old tricks. There was nothing to buy in Australia and the settlers were unable to grow anything. Before long, the new colony, existing on ships' supplies, was on half-rations and in real trouble.

About 30 months after the first settlers landed, a new ship appeared in the harbor. Those on shore hoped it carried a new supply of food. Instead, it carried more convicts, many of them aged and ill, and they only added to the misery of the colony. But fortunately, the Second Fleet, carrying food, new seed, more animals, and healthy reinforcements of people, followed not far behind and the colony was saved.

A total of about 160,000 convicts from England, including many rebellious Irish, were sent to Australia before transportation officially ended in 1868. Very few of the convicts were women, so from the beginning Australia was a heavily male society.

In the earliest decades, naval officers had full authority to govern the settlement of Sydney. Some were cruel to the convicts under their control and to the Aborigines. Many were more interested in their own welfare than the colony's, and they shaped laws to make profits for themselves.

The convicts, hard to control, found it easy to flee the corrupt administration of the Sydney colony. Many of them went into the countryside, found land they could live on, and took possession of it as squatters. Some of them, too, built ranches and farms from which they made good livings and sometimes fortunes.

Between the convicts and the greedy administrators, there was as much disorder as order in the early years of colonization. To that can be added the dangers and disappointments that could be expected in a new and strange land.

Making Order Out of Chaos

The first sense of real order came in 1810. Lachlan Macquarie was appointed governor of the colony of New South Wales, with Sydney as its headquarters. Macquarie broke the monopolies of the naval administrators, or "rum corps," established the first Australian currency and the first bank, and encouraged public works and town planning. Also at this time, free settlers, people who were not criminals, were encouraged to come to Australia.

Meanwhile, the first Australians were beginning to learn a few things about their adopted home. George Bass, a naval surgeon, and Matthew Flinders, a naval officer, sailed out in 1795 to explore the great coastlines. In 1798 they sailed around Tasmania, proving it was an island. In 1801, Flinders was given permission to mount an expedition to chart the entire coast of Australia. He sailed for three years and when he was finished, England and the colonists knew for certain that Australia was an island— there was water on all sides.

Finally, the world knew that this was indeed the long-hidden great southern land. It was finally and officially given the name Australia, an adaptation of the old name Terra Australis Incognita.

Exploring Unknown Land

Meanwhile, the settlers were also curious about the interior of Australia. Macquarie, in addition to everything else he did for the new colony, encouraged exploration inland. Before his term in office ended in 1821, a milestone was passed. The crossing of the Blue Mountains, a difficult natural barrier about 100 miles (about 160 kilometers) inland from Sydney, took place in 1813. Farmers and ranchers had spread out north and south of Sydney. Parramatta, at the western end of Sydney Harbor, was a wonderfully fertile farming area. But the mountains had kept settlement hemmed in until this time.

Other early explorers followed the major rivers of New South Wales. In 1830, Charles Sturt set out with a party on the Murrumbidgee River. He then followed the Lachlan and the Murray rivers. Because rivers flowed west, it was assumed that they emptied into a great inland sea. This would promise a fertile middle country. Sturt got as far as Lake Alexandria, near present-day Adelaide, but he found no inland sea. His party was forced back the way it had come, against the rivers' currents. Sturt, having suffered from heat stroke, dehydration, and fever, was left temporarily blind by the experience. Other explorers clung to the idea that there had to be an inland sea in the interior, but like Sturt they found only disappointment or death.

While Sturt and others suffered heroically, expansion was taking place along the coasts, which were reachable by sailing vessels. Port Phillip, where Melbourne would be built beginning in 1835, was first settled in 1803. A settlement was started on Tasmania the following year. In 1825 the Bathurst and Melville islands off the north coast were claimed as English property. In 1827 a permanent and lonely settlement was begun on the coast of the Indian Ocean at Albany, the first settlement of Western Australia.

Adelaide's first settlers arrived in 1835, the same year as Melbourne's. In 1829, Captain James Stirling (who had already had a look at the Swan River, which empties into the Indian Ocean on the west coast) led the settlers who would build the city of Perth.

Resourceful Colonists

In the early years each of these colonies existed on steadfastness, resourcefulness, and little else. Australians were still trying to adjust to a new climate and harsh new surroundings. Occasionally they had trouble with Aborigines. Sometimes disease spread quickly.

But everywhere the explorers went, people followed, driven by the instinct to be free and the prospect of owning their own land. The rule was that people could have whatever land they claimed. These settlers were called squatters. There was no previous owner to be paid, and Australia provided more than enough land for everyone. The squatters weren't at all sure what could be raised on their land, but at least it was theirs.

It was John MacArthur, once a Sydney administrator, who found a use for the vast interior and who fueled the squatters' rush for land. MacArthur had been a farmer as well as a naval officer. He thought the climate and foliage of the scrubland between the sea and the interior deserts resembled those of Spain, where sheep thrived and supported a wool industry. MacArthur imported merino sheep from Spain, and they proved him right. Not only could these animals tolerate the heat of the interior, but they also could survive in areas where the grass was thin and the soil too rocky for farming. MacArthur's merinos were of supreme importance. They gave Australia its first economy and also the first indication that the hardship of settlement might be worth something.

Oddly enough, the camel was important to Australia's history as well. Camels, not native to Australia, were imported from Afghanistan. For years before there were real roads, they carried supplies to the settlements deep in the Red Center. Horses had quickly failed the early explorers, so they turned to camels, which were used to living in arid deserts.

Eventually, Australians developed a cattle industry. There was some whaling along the coasts. Wheat farming was tried and it, too, expanded until it became an important industry.

While Australians learned what to do with the land under their feet, such explorers as Edward John Eyre and Robert O'Hara Burke pressed farther and farther

Today, farming is very important to Australia's economy. Crops grow in the green and hilly farmland near Melbourne.

Setting up camps to pan gold, people flocked to Australia in search of riches in the days of the gold rush.

inland for a look at the land still unmapped. The idea of a fertile middle area still attracted them. Some journeyed forth and never returned. The explorers who survived won lasting fame. But the answer they brought back was the same one that Sturt had returned with. There was no inland sea watering a fertile center. The center was a terrible desert, unbelievably hostile to humans.

Then this harsh land delivered a surprise. As worthless as much of it appeared on the surface, it was rich underneath. Gold was discovered in 1851 in Bathurst, west of Sydney, and the discovery brought profound change.

Sailors and clerks left their posts in the cities and the ports and headed for Bathurst. Melbourne is said to have almost emptied of men during the gold rush. By July of 1851, rich gold mines were in operation in towns such as Bendigo and Ballarat, and a boom was on. Word spread beyond Australia, and thousands and thousands of new immigrants flocked Down Under to get in on the riches.

INDEPENDENCE AT LAST

In 1868 the transportation of convicts from England stopped, and Australia began to take stock of itself. There were six separate colonies: New South Wales, Victoria, South Australia, Queensland, Western Australia, and Tasmania. Each was separately chartered by Great Britain, and not much cooperation existed between the colonies. The British government appointed governors for the colonies and closely supervised the laws and development of each colony. Beginning about 1875, Britain started to extend a little freedom to the colonies by giving them self-governing status. After this, the colonies could organize their own elections and write laws for themselves, but always under the watchful eye of London.

Finally, Queen Victoria announced that Australia would receive status as a nation on January 1, 1901. The new country would be a full-fledged commonwealth within the British Empire, made up of all its six colonies.

Australia's first constitution was fairly limited. Great Britain would continue to handle Australia's foreign affairs. Laws passed in London would take priority over Australia's own laws; if there was a conflict, London law ruled. Australia could set up its own courts, but anyone who didn't like the ruling of an Australian judge could appeal the decision to a British one. Independence was a big step, and like a toddler, Australia did not stray far from Mother England's skirts. For years after achieving its independence, the country's national anthem remained "God Save the Queen." At last, many years later, in 1984, the country chose its own anthem, "Advance Australia Fair."

World War I

Great Britain expected Australia's help in its wars, and Australia did not fail it. Aussies fought in the Boer War in South Africa on Great Britain's side and, a decade later, in 1914, they joined the British and other Allies in fighting World War I.

World War I gave birth to the ANZACs, as the soldiers of the Australian and New Zealand Army Corps were called. The two countries combined their forces. The first group of them stopped in Egypt on their way to the trenches of France and Belgium. Along with the British, French, and other colonial troops, they were assembled into a force that was ordered to land on the Gallipoli Peninsula and drive the Turkish enemy toward the Black Sea. The invasion was poorly planned, and the Allied forces were pinned down on the beaches for weeks. Thirty-five thousand Allies died, and 3,500 of them were ANZACs. But many more were to die in the trenches of

In Palestine, Aussie troops line up from the Ninth Australian Division in World War I.

Europe. In all, the Australians killed in World War I totaled about 60,000, a shocking number for a new nation.

World War II

After the war, in the 1930s, the world economy slumped, and so did Australia's. Nearly one third of the work force was unemployed, and many companies went bankrupt. Great Britain declared war on Germany again in

1939, at the outset of World War II. And again, Australia answered the call of the empire. ANZACs fought in North Africa and in the Mediterranean. But World War II was different, because this time Australia itself was in danger. The Japanese entered the war in 1941 with their attack on Pearl Harbor. They soon overran much of Asia and the Pacific, and Australia had to think of itself. When Japanese aircraft bombed Australia's Darwin in 1942, the threat of invasion seemed real. England, under attack at home, could not help Australia, but the United States could.

A wartime partnership and a lasting friendship sprang up between the Aussies and the Yanks, who fought alongside each other at the important battle of the Coral Sea and also when the Japanese were rolled back almost island by island in the Pacific.

At home, Australia flourished after World War II. There was an explosion of growth around the world. Most nations, having weathered the Great Depression of the 1930s only to be thrown into war, at last celebrated peace. Those countries which suffered the most during the war were rebuilt. All were hungry customers for the raw materials and agricultural products that Australia supplied in abundance.

After World War II, Australia, New Zealand, and the United States signed a mutual defense agreement called the ANZUS Treaty. In it, each agreed to help the other if any

was attacked in the Pacific. Australia, like most other countries in the world, became a member of the United Nations, which held out the hope that there might never be more attacks anywhere. But there were more wars, although they were smaller. Australian troops lined up with the Americans again during the Korean and Vietnam wars.

With World War II, the world entered the nuclear age. The strain of the invention of nuclear weapons eventually ended the ANZUS partnership. New Zealand was ushered out in 1986. Its government refused to allow United States Navy ships armed with nuclear weapons or powered by nuclear engines to call at its ports any longer. Those who wish to freeze the production of nuclear weapons have urged the Australian government to enact the same ban, thus far without success. But Australia has strictly limited the mining of uranium, and it agreed in 1985 to designate the entire South Pacific region a nuclear-free zone. Whether Australia and the United States remain close friends and allies probably depends somewhat on the course of nuclear politics.

The Immigrants Pour In

Australia needed to increase its population after the war to regain strength as a nation. Hoping to do just that, Australia opened its doors to European immigrants in the

People gather in Canberra on ANZAC Day to remember the soldiers killed in war.

1940s. The government began a special program to encourage homeless European war victims to find shelter in Australia. So many moved to Australia that by the time the 1940s ended, Australia was beginning to come out of its geographic isolation.

Before this time Australia had been a mostly British country with British people. The flood of Italians, Greeks, Germans, Dutch, and Yugoslavs changed the entire social structure of Australia. More than 2 million people came between 1945 and 1965. They provided much of the work force in the 1950s and 1960s—developing factories, mines, roads, and steelworks. Today, one quarter of Australia's population is immigrants and their children.

Up until the 1970s, Australia had a "whites only" immigration policy that excluded all Asians from entering the country. Since then, many have come to Australia from China and Southeast Asia. Now about one third of Australian immigrants are Asian. Australia has always had trade relations with this part of the world, and the South Pacific region is becoming increasingly important in world trade.

Australia's Changing Economy

In recent years, Australia has undergone a major trade shift. In the past, Australia's main economy was based on sheep, wheat, and other agricultural products. Government officials have worried that Australia's raw materials will become less important to customer nations that seem to be turning more to technology for strength. Now, Australia's most valuable resources are uranium and other manufactured products.

In the past, Great Britain was Australia's biggest trade customer. Since the 1960s, Australia has spread its trade to other countries. Japan is now Australia's chief trade partner. It buys coal, iron ore, minerals, wheat, and wool. The United States is the second biggest customer, buying beef, sugar, and bauxite. Australia's neighbor country, New Zealand, also trades with Australia.

By world standards, Australians have a high standard of living and great freedom of lifestyles. Unfortunately, the lucky land is not without its problems. There is ongoing unemployment, and the gap between rich and poor is often great.

The government struggles to bolster the existing economy and to maintain the sense of freedom and prosperity that Australians have come to enjoy. The tourist industry is booming as more and more people learn about Australia from movies about the bush life and the sparkling seashores. But Australia is more than a land of swagmen and kangaroos!

5

THE NATURAL AUSTRALIA

Australia has many distinctive animals. Some, like the koala and the kangaroo, are found nowhere else in the world. Most experts believe this is due to Australia's isolation. Because the continent is surrounded by the sea on all sides, Australia's animal species evolved there and there alone and could not travel to other lands. Most of Australia's animals are not valuable sources of either food or labor, so they were not transported to other countries when white settlers landed.

No one is sure where the kangaroo came from, and no one is sure if kangaroos ever lived anywhere besides in Australia and on a few surrounding islands. Kangaroos are marsupials, mammals that give birth to underdeveloped young. Because they need time to grow, the babies must be carried in the mother's pouch, where they nurse for several months after they are born. The kangaroos' young, for as long as they ride about in the pouch, are called joeys.

Different types of marsupials exist in North and South America and in Asia. Experts say that in those places, they did not have the time to develop as they did in Australia, a continent that lay largely unpopulated for many centuries.

A kangaroo sits with its joey in its pouch.

Australia has 125 separate species of marsupials, ranging from tiny mice to the big red kangaroo, which stands more than 6 feet tall.

The Kangaroo

Of all the marsupials, the kangaroo is the best known. It has become practically a symbol of Australia. A kangaroo wearing boxing gloves appeared on the sails of Australia's challenge boat in the 1983 America's Cup races. When the boat won, this "boxing kangaroo" appeared on tea towels, coffee mugs, T-shirts, tote bags, swimsuits, and license plates.

More than 40 separate varieties of kangaroos live in Australia, including the brawny big red, the half-sized wallaby, and even smaller breeds. They all run with the same distinctive hop. They are much faster than it appears they would be, and city-dwelling Australians and travelers get very excited when they see them. When a herd of kangaroos, all in a line, hop a fence to cross a country road, the sight resembles a ballet performed by gifted acrobats.

Yet kangaroos are a terrible nuisance. They dash into the roads without looking and are a serious hazard to drivers. Practically everyone who lives in the rural districts has hit a kangaroo while driving at night. Most of the people in small towns put special iron bars over the fronts of their cars and trucks to protect against collisions with kangaroos. Some install heavy screens over the windshields, since many kangaroos are big enough to badly damage a vehicle and injure its occupants.

Kangaroos are herbivores, which means they eat grass, seeds, and leaves. In dry weather they gather near the roads to eat in the grassy ditches. It is not unusual to find the roadsides littered with dead kangaroos in the morning during these periods, all of them killed by cars and trucks.

To farmers and ranchers, kangaroos are a serious pest. They eat grass meant for the sheep and also eat and trample crops. Big ones break down fences, letting a farmer's sheep roam into other pastures. Each year, by permission of the government, hunters shoot thousands and thousands of kangaroos just to keep a balance between them and the sheep and cattle. Some farmers and ranchers don't think the official kangaroo kill goes far enough, so they go out on their own unauthorized hunts and kill more. Animal lovers complain about this, but the kangaroo population is so large that most varieties are not really in any danger of extinction.

Other Aussie Mammals

The koala, which also nurses its young in a pouch after birth, is as cuddly as it looks and is gentle, too. It has long claws because it lives in trees and must be able to climb, but it pulls in its claws when it is handled. The koala is a fussy animal. It lives in the branches of the eucalyptus tree, eating leaves from which it gets both food and water. The koala's Aboriginal name means "one who doesn't drink." Australia has 500 to 600 different varieties of eucalyptus, and the koala will eat only the leaves of the kind of tree in which it was born. If a koala finds itself in the wrong kind of eucalyptus tree, it will starve rather than try a new diet. Because the koala has poor eyesight, in daylight as well as in darkness, it has a hard time finding its way home if it is lost. Koalas stay in their trees almost all the time. If they come down, it is at night, and then they do not wander very far.

When early Australians discovered the koala and learned how soft its fur was, they hunted it so vigorously that there was fear for its survival. Finally, the government passed strict laws prohibiting koala hunting and protecting its habitat. Koalas still live in the forests of eastern Australia, free and wild. They are not easy to find, since they hide in their trees. But in the special koala parks near most of the big cities, you can watch them climb, eat, and sleep. You can even pet them!

The wombat is another Australian marsupial. It is a husky, longhaired animal built close to the ground like a pig. It burrows underground, and it eats roots and leaves. Although the wombat is not cute like the koala or

A sleepy koala gets attention in a koala park near Sydney.

Wombats are husky animals that can measure up to four feet long.

The egg-laying duck-billed platypus is one of Australia's strangest native animals.

acrobatic like the kangaroo, it deserves mention because it is another animal found only in Australia.

Monotremes are primitive mammals that lay eggs. Australia has two monotremes, the echidna, or spiny anteater, and the platypus. The echidna, with its coarse brown hair and sharp spines, looks something like a hedgehog. It lives on termites and ants. The platypus has a thick coat of brown fur, webbed feet, and a ducklike bill. It lives along western Australia's streams, rivers, and lakes. This unusual animal uses its long bill to scoop up worms, small shellfish, and other animals as it swims along. As endangered species, both the echidna and the platypus are protected and cannot be hunted or captured without the government's authorization.

The dingo is Australia's famous wild dog. It is believed that the dingo was brought to the continent by the Aborigines when they themselves migrated from Southeast Asia. Dingoes are Australia's chief beasts of prey and among the country's few meat-eating animals. They will attack sheep, cattle, and kangaroos. Dingoes are rust-colored and mean-looking, and their wailing howls can be frightening.

Reptiles

Australia is full of reptiles, including 140 species of snakes and 370 species of lizards. Reptiles, particularly the great monitor, or goanna, lizards, figure importantly in Aboriginal culture. Along a highway south of Darwin is a low, tilted rock formation that resembles the monitor lizard. Tribes of the area believe that the spirit that created the earth adopted the shape of the monitor after its work was done and now lives in that rock. The rock is a protected, sacred site. Goannas 6 feet in length have been captured alive. The lizard that appears on more postcards than any other is the unusual frill-necked lizard of the desert. When it senses danger, flaps alongside its head extend, and the lizard looks as if it is wearing a high ruffled collar.

A crocodile sits along the Adelaide River in the Northern Territory.

Crocodiles live in the bays and coastal rivers of the Northern Territory and Queensland. The crocodiles are very dangerous reptiles, and every year human lives are lost to them. They will bump people out of canoes and flatboats and will snatch them off the banks.

Australia's Native Birds

Many visitors to Australia are surprised at its immense variety of bird life. In fact, Australia has around 700 species of native birds. The countryside is full of eagles, hawks, geese, egrets, cockatoos, and many others,

Emus, as big as ostriches, strut through the countryside.

including parrots. They range in size from the emu, which resembles the ostrich and towers over the tallest kangaroo, to the tiny lily walker, smaller than a child's fist.

Emus stroll around the countryside, usually in pairs, troubling neither man nor beast. They are fun to watch. They look silly, with their very thin legs, fat bodies, and long thin necks, but they are very dignified-looking at the same time. Emus are also very social creatures. If you wave to them from your car, they will walk over and peer in to see if they know you. Emu eggs, bigger than grapefruits, were prized by Aborigines, who would cook the insides after carefully removing them from the shells. The eggshells, preserved whole, are almost leathery. Today, Aborigines carve designs and pictures on the shells, and these are sold in souvenir shops.

The lily walker is found along the ponds and streams of the Northern Territory. The female lays her eggs on a lily pad, and it is the male's job to protect them. When something makes waves that rock the lily pad—perhaps a goose landing or a crocodile entering the water—the male races furiously around the edges of the lily pad, keeping it level and preventing the eggs from rolling into the water.

Other birds are unique to Australia as well. One is the kookaburra. Known for its noisy cackle, it is generally called the laughing kookaburra. Australia's entry in the 1987 America's Cup race at Perth was named

The kookaburra has a large head and long bill. Its call sounds like a loud laugh.

Kookaburra, after this bird. The galah (pronounced gah LAH) is a white bird about the size of a pigeon. Galahs are everywhere in the Outback, always traveling in great flocks. When something spooks them and the whole group rises from the earth, you can see that they have bright pink feathers under their wings. When they fly off, the galahs seem to streak the sky with pink.

Australia even has penguins—a variety known as fairy penguins. They live on the beaches of Phillip Island off Melbourne. At dusk they come ashore and return to the sandy burrows where they live. Many Australians and tourists as well go to Phillip Island just to see the little penguins come home every evening.

Australian Flora

The variety of trees, plants, and flowers is almost endless in Australia. Eucalyptus trees thrive in practically every soil and climate of the country. They are also known as gum trees, and varieties range from bushes shorter than the average human to towering giants. Many of the gums are recognizable by their swollen trunks and gnarled, twisted limbs. Acacia trees, particularly the variety known as the mulga, are also found all over Australia. In northern Queensland there are rain forests where trees are jungle-thick and hung with vines and creepers. In the

deserts, trees are few and far between. The few that are there look dwarfed and barely nourished, as if they are struggling to survive.

One tree found in Australia, the southern beech, is also found in South America and South Africa. The reason that the same tree is found in three different parts of the world, scientists believe, is that much of the Southern Hemisphere was once all one landmass, not separated by oceans as its parts are today.

Wildflowers grow all over Australia, and in the scrubland and the deserts they put on an extraordinary show. These empty deserts are dull and colorless in the dry seasons, as if all life were parched out of them. Trees and grass dry up and begin to turn brown. With a downpour the picture changes dramatically. Green reappears as if by magic, and all over the landscape, wildflowers bloom in great numbers. Red and pink, blue and white, orange and yellow, they blanket the countryside. It is a glorious sight.

Gum trees such as this one are found throughout Australia. The old local name for this tree is the blue gum, but it is also known as the forest red gum.

Australia Celebrates

Australians love to celebrate, and their calendar is full of holidays, festivals, and commemorations. Some, such as Christmas, New Year's Day, and Easter, are celebrated much as Americans celebrate them. Some are British holidays and are celebrated in all the countries that once made up the British Empire. Other holidays are purely Australian.

For Aussies Only

The two main Australia-only holidays have fixed dates, and everyone celebrates them at the same time. One is joyous, and the other is solemn. Australia Day, the happy occasion, is celebrated on January 26. It commemorates the arrival of the first white settlers aboard the First Fleet of Captain Phillip in 1788. This was modern Australia's beginning, and this holiday evokes memories of everything Australian.

On Australia Day the landing at Sydney Harbor is reenacted. Children dress up in historical costumes and play famous people from the past in pageants throughout the country. Special concerts celebrate Australia's musical talent. Sporting contests and tournaments add to the festivity.

Spectators watch a reenactment of the arrival of the First Fleet in Sydney Harbor at the Australia Day celebration in 1988.

One of the biggest Australia Day celebrations ever took place in 1988, because that was the two hundredth anniversary of the arrival of the first white settlers. The highlight of the celebrations in 1988 was the dedication of the new national capitol buildings in Canberra.

The solemn commemoration is ANZAC Day, which occurs on April 25 of every year. It honors the many men who fought and died overseas for Australia and for

England. Surviving veterans parade in their old uniforms, and the former commanders make speeches. Trumpeters play sad salutes to the fallen. The Boer War is remembered, as are the Gallipoli invasion and the trenches of France and Belgium. Men from the days of World War II talk about the Desert Campaign in Africa and the terrible fighting against the Japanese on the Kokoda Trail in New Guinea. Younger men recall the Korean War and Vietnam. ANZAC Day is a reminder that progress often demands sacrifice. Every year speakers express the wish that the world will one day learn to progress without more wars.

Other National Holidays

Another major holiday remembers the British Empire and Australia's part in it. This is Commonwealth Day, celebrated in May every year. When the British Empire was dissolved after World War II, roughly over the years from 1948 to 1965, it was replaced by the British Commonwealth. The nations that made up the empire were, one by one, granted total self-rule and independence. But they all have common ties to England, and they continue to meet as equals to discuss world affairs among themselves.

Although no single country can tell the others what to do, they feel they can perhaps be a force for good and for peace in the world. Queen Elizabeth II of the United Kingdom is a great supporter of the Commonwealth and takes her honorary position as head of it very seriously. The 49 nations of the Commonwealth meet in a different country every year, most of them represented by their highest officials.

Labor Day, although it is much the same the world over, has special meaning in Australia, where the man who digs a ditch is as proud of what he does as the businessman who makes million-dollar deals. Every working man and woman celebrates Labor Day in Australia. Just as in America, it is a day of speeches, politics, and picnics. Labor Day is celebrated on many different dates in Australia—depending on the area.

Some sporting events are occasions for public holidays in Australia. Adelaide Cup Day is a holiday that celebrates a big horse race. Melbourne Cup Day is a public holiday so that everyone can spend the day watching the horse race. Once a year the small Outback town of Alice Springs hosts a camel race, and tourists can see many camels on the nearby camel farms.

Australia's Cultural Blend

The many immigrants from other lands and other cultures have enriched the Australian calendar with new

*The finish of the Melbourne Cup horse races is an
exciting moment for all the spectators.*

holidays and festivals. Chinese New Year, although not a day off from work or school, is celebrated wherever the Chinese find themselves. It is a festival of food and entertainment. Historically, it is also a time when the Chinese settle any debts they have and start anew.

Hungarians commemorate their unsuccessful 1956 uprising against their Communist government every October. In Australia as well as in America, it is a sad day of remembrance. Other people, such as the Greeks and the Italians, have their own celebrations as well. Some are religious, centering around the churches. All add to the flavor of the new and worldly Australia.

The famous traditional festivals of the Aborigines are called corroborees (kah ROB oh reez). A corroboree might be held in celebration, perhaps, for deliverance from a drought or other danger. It might be a religious festival, held in honor of the guarding spirits. Often it marks the initiation of young boys into full manhood.

Aborigine men take the main roles at corroborees. They paint their bodies and they dance. They are skilled at mimicking the movements of animals. Corroborees might include sporting contests to see who can throw a spear the farthest and straightest or who can make a boomerang do the most tricks. Music at corroborees usually comes from a didgeridoo, a long hollow tube played by mouth that makes a mournful sound.

*Playing the didgeridoo and dancing, these Aborigines participate
in their traditional festival, the corroboree.*

Women usually have a secondary role at corroborees. They prepare the feast, and they might attend as part of the audience, but the performances are left to the men. When a corroboree involves initiation for young boys, only men and boys attend. Women hold their own initiation ceremonies for young girls, and men are forbidden to attend these.

The corroboree is almost always a private celebration, open only to members of a particular tribe of Aborigines. However, Aborigines perform their traditional dances and play the didgeridoo for tourists at various Outback hotels and other locations, so everyone can get a glimpse of the ceremony.

Christian Holidays and New Year's Day

Christmas is celebrated on December 25 and is the time when people celebrate the birth of Christ. It is also a chance for families to gather together and is a time of major gift-giving to family, friends, and loved ones. People take short holidays then, and children are out of school.

But there is one big difference in the Australian Christmas. December 25 in Australia falls in summer because the seasons are the opposite of those in the United States. Many Australians make it a tradition to go to the beach on Christmas, while many Americans might go outdoors in the snow. Family Christmas pictures in Australia often show a Christmas tree stuck in the sand and the family grouped around it. Father Christmas comes to the beach (sometimes in shorts), and the gifts he leaves are wrapped in paper that shows reindeer in the snow. Everything about an Australian Christmas would be familiar to Americans except for the summer weather.

The day after Christmas in Australia and all the Commonwealth countries is called Boxing Day. Boxing Day, traditionally, is the day when people used to put their leftovers from Christmas in boxes for the poor. Now, people leave small gifts or tips for the mail carrier, the person who delivers newspapers, the grocer, and the butcher. These are little gifts to say thank you for good service.

Boxing Day is an old English custom. The coming of labor unions, which guarantees a minimum wage for most working people, has removed some of the original reasons for Boxing Day. Even people who do errands no longer have to depend on tips. However, no one likes to let go of a holiday once it is established, and Boxing Day continues. Since most people do not have to work on Boxing Day, the stores are usually full, and the day marks the beginning of the big after-Christmas sales.

Fireworks light up Sydney Harbor on New Years' Eve.

Easter, as in the rest of the world, usually takes place on a different Sunday each year, depending on the church calendar. As in the United States, Easter is an important religious occasion, marking the Resurrection of Christ. Of course, Good Friday and Easter come in the autumn in Australia. Children sometimes dye Easter eggs as American children do, but it is much more common for them to hunt for chocolate eggs or Easter baskets.

New Year's Day is January 1 and is another summer holiday in Australia. As everywhere else, it is a time to remember the year just past and to start a new one. Australians are optimistic people, and the beginning of a new year is something they celebrate with great hope and enthusiasm.

ALL THE COMFORTS OF HOME

Three out of four Australians live in cities, most of them in the green and sunny belt of coastline that runs from Brisbane on the eastern coast to Adelaide on the southern coast. Despite all the attention the Outback gets, Australia is one of the most urbanized countries in the world. The typical Australian city layout—a tiny central city surrounded by a number of residential or suburban areas— is found throughout the British Commonwealth countries. All of them copied London, England, the principal city of the old British Empire. London has a small "city" area with Greater London spread around it. All the big Australian cities—Sydney, Brisbane, Melbourne, Adelaide, Perth, and Darwin—are laid out on this plan. The design is even the same in smaller cities like Alice Springs, which is the main city of the Outback but has fewer than 30,000 residents.

Suburban Sydney

Sydney, the country's largest city, is a good example of a sprawling, heavily populated coastal area. Its downtown (the actual "city of Sydney") is quite small in area, occupying only about 15 square miles (about 24 square

Sparkling Sydney (next two pages) is a coastal city that stretches inland and is surrounded by suburbs.

kilometers). Here, skyscrapers stand on the slope of land rising from the harbor where the first settlers landed. All around this small downtown area spread the suburbs and far suburbs that make up greater Sydney. Sydney reaches more than 100 miles (160 kilometers) north and south along the Pacific coast. It stretches more than 50 miles (80 kilometers) west to the Blue Mountains.

This sprawling city includes 31 separate municipalities and many, many more residential communities. It covers over 3,000 square miles (4,800 square kilometers), and it offers residents of Sydney many choices of living styles.

Many residents of Sydney live on the water. Not only is there the Pacific coastline, but Sydney Harbor itself extends inland for miles. Waterfront homes are prized, and this is where some of Sydney's most expensive areas are found.

Outside of downtown Sydney, the suburbs cluster together, one after the other, across land that is sometimes flat, sometimes rolling. There are communities of every character. Some are built around modern shopping centers; others resemble old-fashioned villages. In some the houses sit close together on city-sized lots, and in others the houses are more spread out. The coastal belt of greater Sydney gets enough rain to keep it green much of the year, and the farthest suburbs have a nice country look.

Most of the communities that make up greater Sydney are complete mini-cities in themselves. They have their own schools, churches, and recreational facilities, and include community business districts and shopping centers.

A modern and very efficient system of commuter trains links Sydney with its far-flung suburbs, and this is how most working people get to downtown jobs. There are no auto expressways as we know them. Still, owning a car is very important to the average Australian, and cars are necessary for people who must get from one suburb to another.

City Housing

Australians believe strongly in a separate house for each family, so there are very few apartment buildings. It is estimated that 75 percent of Australians buy their own homes. Most of the newer Australian homes are one-story buildings made of wood and brick, or wood and stone. Americans would call them ranch houses. Australia is a country of low buildings; in fact, it did not have sky-scrapers until the 1950s. Most suburban homes in Australia are surrounded by lawns and have attached garages.

An earlier type of Australian home is found in the close-in residential areas of cities like Sydney. These are

These houses cover the hills of Melbourne, and are typical of Australian architecture.

all-wood homes and they have two distinct features—they have low porches one step up from the ground across the entire front of them, and they are decorated with trellislike trim. Since housing lots are smaller in the older parts of the cities, these homes are usually close together with only a narrow walkway separating one from another.

New or old, Australian homes have one thing in common: The most important room in the house is the living room. Australians call it the lounge. A typical Australian lounge will include a comfortable couch or two, several chairs, a large table, a television, a bookcase, and often a mantel displaying the family photographs.

The lounge is where everyone gathers at the end of the day. Children do their homework at the table, and the couch is always placed for the best television viewing. The family always entertains visitors in the lounge and sometimes eats meals there as well. A house without a good-sized lounge wouldn't seem a house at all to many Australians.

Entertainment in the City

In Sydney, places where families enjoy entertainment range from the Opera House to the cabaret theaters (where Australia's sassy humor is exhibited) to rock-and-roll clubs. Its many movie theaters present the best films from around the world, as well as the many fine films made in Australia. The main libraries and museums are near the city center. The Rocks, the actual point where the first settlers landed, has been transformed from an aging, dirty warehouse district into a showplace of shops and restaurants. At Circular Quay, Sydney residents board ferryboats that carry them across the harbor to the Sydney Zoo or up and down the harbor on excursion rides. There are many fine restaurants, so many that people say you can find any cuisine of the world in the city of Sydney.

Australia's other cities offer similar types of amusement and entertainment. Each of Australia's state capitals has a permanent company of professional actors who perform classical and modern plays year-round, as well as a professional symphony orchestra. The Australian Opera and the Australian Ballet also keep the Aussies entertained.

Outback Living

Life in the Outback is much different from city life. Immense distances separate places in the Great Empty. Cities are few and far between, and the towns are very small. Sheep ranches and farms can be many thousands of acres in size, and the people who live on them may get to town only once a week and to major cities no more than once or twice a year.

The Outback is full of interesting rock formations. These mystical rocks, called Olgas, are known as Heads to the Aborigines.

Farm and ranch homes in the Outback tend to be large, sprawling places because they have to serve many purposes. One part of the house contains the office of the farm or ranch. Homes have to be big enough to accommodate overnight company, since almost every visitor stays the night. Each house has large storerooms and pantries because farm families have to stock up heavily on food and supplies when they shop in town. Most farms and ranches have family gardens where families grow some food for their own use.

Since towns are so far away, farm and ranch families must provide their own entertainment. Many homes have swimming pools. Indoors, there might be billiard tables and ping-pong tables. People living in the Outback have television, just as city residents do, though they don't receive as many channels. Videocassette recorders, or VCRs, are popular. When nothing is on television, Outback families will show home and feature movies or videotapes of family weddings and other occasions.

The vast countryside itself provides many opportunities for recreation. Families hunt and even fish if they are near a river that flows year-round. They ride horses and sometimes take motorbikes on trail rides. When many friends and relatives gather for a big picnic, ranch hands will often go out and corral two kangaroos of equal size. Then the highlight of the picnic will be kangaroo races.

An outback child and her lamb. There are more sheep than people in Australia!

When ranch families go to town, a lot of the trip's enjoyment comes from just visiting with town friends and catching up on the news. Most small towns have a movie theater. Almost every town has a chapter of the Returned Servicemen's League, an organization much like the American Legion. Often its clubhouse is the center of social activity for the area.

Australians living on ranches and farms in the Outback rely heavily on each other. Homesteads are linked by two-way radio. Families share vital information, such as the condition of roads and wildfire warnings, and they pass on emergency calls in case of illness or accidents. One homestead in every region has a landing strip where the Royal Flying Doctor Service, which provides the Outback with emergency ambulance transportation, can land its planes. In the Red Center, the mail carrier is a pilot who flies out with the mail once a week, landing at each ranch to deliver letters, have a cup of tea, and share the news and gossip.

Vehicles are extremely important in the Outback, and it is vital that they be kept in tiptop condition. If someone is badly hurt and must be driven to a landing strip to meet the flying doctors, a truck's failure to start could be fatal. Everybody who drives in the Outback must be part mechanic, just as someone at every isolated homestead must be part doctor.

*Many Outback vehicles look like this off-road van–
packed to the top with emergency equipment.*

Workers on a sheep ranch in New South Wales are busy shearing the wool from the sheep to sell around the world.

When people leave a sheep ranch or farm to drive into town, they call first to say they are coming. If they do not arrive and check in by a certain time, the people in town go out looking for them in case there has been an accident or a vehicle has broken down. A breakdown in the desert, particularly in the awful heat of summer, can be fatal. This is why it is common to see cars with extra tires strapped to their roofs, spare fanbelts dangling from the mirrors, and cans of gasoline and drinking water loaded in the back seats.

The Outback is a long, lonely way from the splendid cities on Australia's coastlines, with their rich variety. Yet there are genuine rewards in the Outback, too. There is room to feel free and to escape from traffic lights and traffic jams.

Making a living in the Outback is hard work. Farming is an uncertain occupation, always at the mercy of the weather. Sheep ranchers work from dawn to dusk in certain seasons and into the night during shearing. Some Outback residents mine gleaming opals. Opal mining can be difficult, as workers dig underground, crank pails of soil to the surface one by one, and sift the soil for jewels.

Living in the Outback can also be very profitable. It is not unusual to meet sheep ranchers or farmers who own their own airplanes, send their children to boarding school, and enjoy an occasional vacation in Europe, Fiji, or Singapore. Not all opal miners get rich, but it is not uncommon for one to reach into a jeans pocket and pull out polished gems worth thousands of dollars.

Eat, Drink, and Be Merry!

Because Australians eat everything from potatoes to kangaroos, it would be difficult to say what the national food is. Australia's many immigrants have brought their cooking traditions along with them to their new home. Today, restaurants featuring Chinese, Japanese, Vietnamese, Italian, Greek, and many other types of cooking offer diners great variety in the country's larger, more cosmopolitan cities.

Australia did, however, inherit many dishes and tastes from the English. In the tradition of England, Aussies like sturdy meals. That means they eat a lot of meat, almost always accompanied by potatoes, baked or boiled. Bread is also a staple of most meals. Australians enjoy English meat pies, which consist of meat and gravy baked in a bread crust. These are available at many restaurants.

Beef is often served as the main course, but equally common is lamb. Every Australian cook, man or woman, can do a thousand things with lamb. One of the most popular dishes, and a delicious one, is curried lamb, usually served as a stew. It is a dish that brings together the Australian national animal, the sheep, with the hot spices of Indonesia and other parts of Asia. Australians will carry a pot of curried lamb to a barbecue or a beach party just the way Americans would take baked beans.

Here is a recipe for lamb curry.

Lamb Curry

2 pounds lamb, any cut except chops
1 tablespoon vegetable shortening or oil
2 tablespoons curry powder
2 cups beef stock (canned stock or stock made from bouillon cubes may be used)
1/2 cup chopped onion
1/2 cup chopped celery
1 tablespoon chopped fresh parsley

Trim the fat from the meat and then cut the meat into chunks. In a large skillet, brown the meat in the shortening or oil over medium heat. Add the beef stock. Stir in the curry powder. Add the onion, the celery, and the parsley. Stir together. Cover the pan and simmer the mixture for 45 minutes. Serve lamb curry in a large soup bowl, with rice or bread.

Some people even eat kangaroo meat. Those who have say it tastes like veal. It is said to be healthier than beef for humans, since it is not as fatty. But kangaroo meat isn't cooked too often in Australian kitchens, and only now and then does a restaurant offer it as a novelty. Kangaroo-tail soup, however, is regarded as something of a delicacy and is served in some fine restaurants.

Although meat dishes are still popular, Australians have recently begun to add more fresh vegetables, fruits, and seafood to their diets. Seafood is in fact one of Australia's best offerings. This is understandable, since the continent is surrounded by water! Sydney rock oysters, Moreton Bay bugs (like small crabs), and large crayfish are standard fare.

Barbecues are something of an Australian tradition and so are beach parties. The country's wonderful climate means great weather for outdoor cooking, and its people make the most of it. Both meat and fish are cooked over open fires. A barbecue in the Northern Territory almost certainly would include both barramundi, an enormous fish caught in northern rivers, and steaks of water buffalo, which tastes like beef. Australians imported water buffalo from Indonesia many years ago as beasts of burden. Now they have become wild and are hunted for their meat.

Bush picnics and cookouts often serve damper bread and billy tea. Damper is made from wheat flour, which is mixed with water and then kneaded. The dough is placed on a heavy cast-iron pot that is then put in a hole in the ground and covered with hot coals to bake. Some people wrap it on a stick and cook it over the coals like a toasted marshmallow. Billy tea is prepared in a tin can over the fire.

Some say that the national drink is tea, as it is in England. Others insist that beer is the national favorite. Over 24 breweries in Australia produce more than 70 kinds of beer. One of the more famous beers is Foster's Lager in the big can, or tinny, as the Australians would call it.

Desserts are as popular in Australia as they are everywhere. One treat unique to Australia is a meringue dessert called the pavlova. A square sponge cake covered with chocolate and coconut is called a lamington. A favorite cookie among Australian children is the "anzac," named for the famous Australian and New Zealand soldiers.

Anzacs

1 cup butter
2 tablespoons maple syrup
1 cup plain flour
1 teaspoon baking powder
1 cup rolled oats
1 cup flaked coconut, unsweetened
1 cup sugar

Soften butter slightly; then cream in with maple syrup. Add the remaining ingredients. Roll into small balls; place well apart on greased baking trays. Bake in moderate oven (350°) for approximately 15 minutes. Cool on tray before removing.

THE AUSTRALIAN CLASSROOM

Australia has as much variety in education as it has in everything else, partly because each Australian state makes its own laws. Since most Australian children live in modern metropolitan areas, they go off to school in the morning and return home in the afternoon, just as American children do. But Australian children who live in rural areas of the Outback hardly ever visit a classroom in their early years.

In either case, attendance in school in Australia is required between the ages of 6 and 15, with the exception of the state of Tasmania, where children must attend school until they are 16. Kindergarten is not required anywhere, but most children start school earlier than kindergarten anyway. Preschool classes are very popular in Australia, and many children start attending them when they are 4 years old.

Public Schools

In the United States we sometimes say that "real school" begins with the first grade. Australians call it year one. Primary education lasts from year one through year

Children in an Australian classroom

six or seven, depending on the area. The emphasis in primary school is on teaching every child to read and write. Students also learn simple arithmetic and history. Some schools, but not many, introduce children to foreign languages in primary school. After primary school, secondary school—what we would call high school—begins.

Uniforms are required in practically every Australian school. They are so common that children are used to wearing them. Secondary schools almost always have dress codes. Although uniforms are not usually required, the dress rules are taken seriously.

Primary-school children usually attend a full day of classes in one classroom, leaving the room only for special activities such as art, music, or gym. Older children, those in their last primary years and those in secondary school, move from classroom to classroom. Some secondary schools are laid out like university campuses. The school day starts at 8:30 A.M. and ends between 3:00 P.M. and 4:00 P.M. After-school activities, such as sports, band, and drama, begin in the late primary years and continue through secondary school.

About 80 percent of all Australian children attend government schools, or public schools. Government schools are free to everyone all the way through secondary school. Nongovernment schools, either private or

Schoolchildren take a break from school to go on a field trip–by train!

religious, charge tuition fees and mostly are owned and operated by the Roman Catholic church. These schools teach the same basic courses that government schools do. Both public- and private-school students receive transportation allowances from the government when they have to travel to their schools.

School—at Home!

The great sheep stations and farms of the Outback are too isolated to permit many country children to get to the classrooms every day. Even when the children live close enough to be driven to school, the roads may not be reliable. Often the trip is so slow and long that some parents decide that the distance is too much for primary-school children.

Outback children usually are taught by their parents at home. Some get their lessons by two-way radio and some by television. Many take their important examinations by mail.

A radio teacher can talk to many children on different sheep stations and farms at the same time. The teacher can't see the students, so they can attend radio class in their pajamas if their parents don't object. But *two-way* means that the teacher can hear as well as talk, so children have to be prepared for their lessons, no matter what they wear. When the teacher asks a question, an answer is expected.

The radio network on which lessons are given is on the same frequency that farmers and ranchers use to pass along emergency messages. Emergency messages have priority over everything else. If they come during classes, radio-school children get the same sort of break that city students get when there are surprise fire or tornado drills.

In the Outback, home tutoring is much more common than any other kind of schooling. One of the children's parents is usually the teacher, although when farm or ranch families can afford it, they sometimes hire a tutor outside the family. Such tutors are usually licensed teachers. Often they are city teachers who want to experience living in the Outback for a while.

Lesson plans for home tutoring are prepared by the government and mailed to Outback homes so that Outback children will be taught the same courses as students in the cities. Workbooks are required. Once a week or so, pages from the children's workbooks are mailed to town. Here they are checked by school administrators to make sure the right work is being done. Home tutoring is sometimes referred to as correspondence school, and the reason is that the schoolwork is sent through the mail.

Depending on the distance and on the weather and road conditions, Outback children who attend school at home are driven to town at least once a month to spend a day with other children in a regular classroom. This way, children can meet with others of their own age. It also allows them to get used to a classroom. When they reach secondary-school age, most Outback children will make the trip to town for classes.

In farm and ranch homes, one room is usually set aside as the children's classroom. The classroom is usually different from the other parts of the house, where the children watch TV or just relax. This is meant to help the children understand that education is important to their futures.

A classroom at home might have all the equipment found in a regular schoolroom, including a chalkboard, wall maps, and school desks. Outback children have a schedule, just as the city-school children do. They report to the classroom after breakfast, go from one subject to another, and break for recess and lunch at the same time every day. The teacher assigns homework and gives tests and quizzes.

Once Outback children reach secondary-school age, they usually are sent to the town schools. If they are close enough, they are driven in each day and home again in the evening. If the distance is too far, the children move into town. Some stay in the homes of family friends, others stay in hostels, or supervised lodging, for students. In this case, it is the ranch or the farm that the children visit only now and then.

Decision Time

In secondary school, students make important decisions about their futures. With the advice of parents and teachers, children have to decide what type of subjects to study. They can learn commercial or technical subjects that prepare them to find work immediately after high school, or they can concentrate on college preparatory subjects. This decision is usually made between years 10 and 11. The great majority of Australian high school students choose to concentrate on vocational subjects. They might study agriculture, animal husbandry, or mechanical trades, or they might study for positions in business offices or jobs in the service industries.

In the mid-1980s, there were only 19 universities in all of Australia. These universities are all publicly owned. There are many more colleges that train people for jobs such as teaching music or public health nursing.

The universities are almost all located in or near the large cities. Admission to them is based on how well the students did in secondary school. The universities offer a full range of studies, from medicine and law to the humanities. Although a growing number of Australian universities operate graduate schools, students who seek advanced degrees usually go abroad. Most go to England, but many go to other countries in Europe or to the United States.

Learning to make small cakes, Aboriginal students take cooking lessons at Koomilda College in Darwin.

Help for the Students

Australia has special programs for the education of Aborigine children and the children of immigrants for whom English is a second language. In some schools, when Aborigine youngsters report for year one, they will find not only an English-speaking teacher but also an Aborigine teacher's-aide who speaks the local tribal dialect. The aide's job is to make the Aborigine children comfortable in the classroom and to help them get used to the idea of learning in English. However, an increasing number of students are leaving school as soon as the law allows them to do so.

New programs are aimed at reducing the high dropout rate of children in secondary school. To encourage Aboriginal students to stay in school, the Australian government often pays their families special allowances to help buy school clothes and other necessities. Sometimes the programs are unsuccessful. In the 1980s about two thirds of all students left school when they were 16 years old. Because of the determination of the teachers and the help of government educational programs, most of today's Australians can read and write. The children of Australia are being taught the importance of a formal education, whether by two-way radio or in the classroom!

SPORTS UNDER THE SUN

When Australia won the America's Cup sailing competition in 1983, the races took place many time zones away in the waters off Newport, Rhode Island. In the past, the Americans were the only ones who had ever won the competition. Back in Australia, there was tremendous excitement. It seems that the entire country stayed up all night to watch a live telecast of the final races.

Prime Minister Bob Hawke went on national television and excused everyone who was late for work or for school the morning after the final race. The America's Cup of 1983 was an exceptional moment. It combined two strong elements of Australian culture—love of country and love of sports.

People all over the world participate in sports and are sports fans. But it is difficult to think of a country that loves sports as much as Australia does. Almost everyone, whether young or old, is active in some sport or outdoor activity. Australia's wonderful climate, with its many days of sunshine, makes the country a perfect place for sports. In addition, many workers are entitled to long vacations—four weeks paid for most and six weeks paid for many. This gives Australians ample free time to devote to their favorite recreation.

Athletes compete in professional matches played in huge stadiums before thousands of spectators and big television audiences, as well as in amateur tournaments played in the tiniest of Outback settlements. Whether the contest is big or small, no one takes the games casually. Australians are serious about their sports, and everyone plays to win. All of Australia's great sporting instincts will be on parade in the year 2000, when Sydney hosts the Summer Olympic Games.

Cricket and Wickets

Cricket, played in the summer, is perhaps the biggest and most popular sport in Australia. It is also the one closest to the hearts of the people, perhaps because the game comes from England and has the oldest tradition associated with it. Cricket clubs meet all over Australia. The best players are chosen for the national team, which represents Australia abroad in international matches against England and other countries that once were part of the British Empire. These international matches, called test matches, are probably the biggest events of the entire Australian sports year. People argue about them months before they happen and then wait almost in silence for the results.

Some people see a similarity between cricket and baseball. Cricket has a pitcher, called a bowler, and a batter, called a batsman. There are fielders. But there is no foul territory. Often the batsman doesn't run after he hits the ball, and it means nothing if the batsman swings and misses. Instead of pitching the ball, the bowler must bounce it to the batsman. Some people think there isn't a lot of resemblance between cricket and baseball after all if one takes a closer look.

Two wickets are set up on the cricket field, one behind the bowler and one behind the batsman. A wicket is made up of three upright wooden sticks, with a wooden slab laid across the top of the sticks. The bowler tries to bounce the ball past the batsman so that the ball, heavier and harder than a baseball, knocks down the wicket. The batsman uses his bat, which is like a long paddle, to defend the wicket by hitting the ball away.

If the batsman hits the ball far enough, he will run to the bowler's wicket and back to his own. Meanwhile, the fielders try to return the ball and hit the wicket before he can complete his run. If he hits the ball beyond the field's boundaries, he scores six runs. If he hits the ball into the air and a fielder catches it before it hits the ground, he is out. He is also out if the bowler bounces one past him and knocks down the wicket.

A skilled batsman can bat for more than an hour, and some matches last for days. The traditional clothing for cricket is white slacks, a white shirt, and white shoes.

A batsman hits a cricket ball on the greens at a game between Victoria and New South Wales.

Each club has caps in its team colors (to go with all that white), and the more colorful the cap, the better.

Club cricket is often an amateur game. The players hold regular jobs and play cricket on weekends. But the higher a player ranks in competition, the more time the game demands of him. Almost all players on the national teams are professionals who are paid for their sport. And almost all cricketeers are men, although women's teams play here and there.

Australia's Football

If cricket, so rich in history and tradition, is the first sport in Australia, then rugby runs a very close second. Rugby, called football or footie by Australians, is played with a leather ball shaped like an oval. The ball looks a lot like an American football, although it is plumper and has rounder ends. There are either 11 or 13 players on a team, depending on the type of rugby being played, and the object of the game is to carry the ball across a points line or to score points by aiming accurate kicks between tall upright poles.

As in American football, players tackle and run into each other. However, there are some genuine differences. Rugby is much faster than American football; its players run almost constantly. Games are practically nonstop, with hardly any timeouts called. The players do not wear protective pads or helmets, but the collisions are just as violent as those in American football.

Rugby at the top professional level draws huge crowds. The top players are paid to play, although almost all of them have regular jobs as well. The country also has amateur leagues. Nearly every town, even the very smallest, fields a town team. When the team plays at home, it is an exciting day and almost everyone attends, or so it seems. When the game is held in another town, the team's fans often make the trip in a caravan, even though the journey might take several hours.

Many young boys who play rugby dream of someday winning a place on the national team, which plays matches with other countries. It is a great honor for athletes to be asked to represent their countries, especially in Australia, where sports are so popular. Rugby matches are always exciting, but when Australia challenges New Zealand's best players, the fans go wild.

Soccer, Lawn Bowling, and Horse Racing

Soccer also attracts many followers in Australia, although it ranks behind cricket and rugby in fan interest. Australia is not one of the world's soccer powers yet, but its supporters hope to develop a national team that will become a strong competitor for the World Cup, the highest prize in soccer.

Australia even has professional lawn bowlers and a national lawn bowling team. In this sport, a white target ball is set in place on a grass court as smooth and slick as a golf putting green. From about 25 yards away, the opposing bowlers roll heavy balls, each trying to get closer to the white ball. Lawn bowling is a very quiet game, but as it is in every other game in Australia, competition is keen.

Horse racing is a gala event in Australia. The Melbourne Cup has become an international classic in thoroughbred racing. The day of the race is a general holiday, with no school and no work in much of the state of Victoria, and huge crowds gather at the track. But horse racing is just as exciting in the small towns and cities of the Outback. Practically every town of any size at all has a racetrack and a yearly racing schedule, if only one or two days long.

Many Australians love to gamble, and bookies wearing huge leather purses over their shoulders set up their betting stands on the grass near the track and call the odds. Townspeople get their best clothes out of mothballs and dress up for the races. Almost everybody gets out to the track, which is usually on the outskirts of town, and farmers and ranchers drive in from their lonely spreads.

Soccer is a popular game throughout Australia.
Here Australia and New Zealand compete in the World Cup.

At the small country tracks, fans can lean over the rail and be close enough to the action to feel the thundering hooves of the horses.

Some Famous Aussie Athletes

Australian athletes are best known to Americans through their participation in individual sports, such as swimming, track, tennis, and golf. During the 1950s, Dawn Fraser held many women's swimming records and was the swimmer to beat in all her races in the Olympics. In 1954, Australian runner John Landy pushed Britisher Roger Bannister to the first ever under-four-minutes mile during the international Empire Games in Vancouver, Canada.

Australians no longer dominate the world tennis scene. But it was not long ago that Australians Lew Hoad, Rod Laver, Ken Rosewall, and John Newcombe all but ruled men's tennis and that Margaret Court Smith and Evonne Goolagong Cawley took the major women's championships.

Evonne Goolagong Cawley is the part-Aborigine tennis player who, at the age of 19, won the tennis championship at Wimbledon, England. Now married and a resident of the United States, she was born in the city of Griffith, 300 miles (480 kilometers) west of Sydney.

The Australian Tennis Open in Melbourne draws large crowds.

She grew up in a large family in the town of Barellan, where her father made his living as a mechanic and a sheep shearer.

One of the most successful golfers in all the world is Greg Norman, an Australian raised in Queensland. Norman has twice won the British Open, one of golf's top tournaments. Another Australian, Ian Baker-Finch, also won the British Open, and David Graham won the U.S. Open. But they all must look up to Peter Thomson, an older golfer who in his heyday won the British Open five times. Jan Stephenson, Penny Pulz, Karen Permezel, and Karrie Webb are Australians who have played on the American women's professional golf tour.

Sunning, Swimming, and Surfing

Every professional sport played in Australia is played for fun as well as pay. The wonderful climate means people can play year-round. In Sydney, for instance, people say that the weather allows them to swim or sail almost every day. Australians are avid sailors, and every major city on the coast stages competitive regattas, or sailing races. Australian sailors participate in international ocean competitions and, of course, in matches like the America's Cup. In many areas the waves are high and the surfing is great. There hardly is a weekend when the cities' harbors aren't full of boats of all kinds.

An underwater photographer snaps photos of several kinds of corals among the waters of the Great Barrier Reef.

The Australians love to explore the wonders of their country. In the Outback, roaming the wide-open spaces is a popular form of recreation. People coming all the way from the coastal cities wander in the great interior in off-road vehicles, on horseback, on camels, by light plane, and even by hot-air balloon.

The Great Barrier Reef is a paradise for divers and swimmers, fishermen and sunbathers. Many islands off the reef have been developed as resorts, particularly in the vicinity of Cairns. Some of these islands are so small that there is barely room for a hotel. When the tide is out, vacationers can walk the reef in protective shoes and examine its shapes and colors. There are beaches everywhere, and thousands of tourists visit every year.

The development of the jet aircraft and then the jumbo jet after World War II has opened up the possibility of easy international travel for Australians, and they take full advantage of the opportunity. Australia is located in an exotic and fascinating part of the world, not far at all from Singapore, Malaysia, Borneo, New Guinea, Fiji, Tahiti, or Bali. Their generous vacation pay helps Australians afford travel to all parts of the world. Australians like nothing better than to be on the go, out of doors, and preferably playing some type of game.

AUSSIES ABROAD

Very few Australians have come to the United States to live. The main reason is that Australia is so much like the United States. Historically, both have offered the same hope of opportunity. They promised their first settlers and the thousands that followed a new chance, room to roam, and new freedoms from old ways.

The one group of Australians that did come to the United States were the war brides of World War II. Many American soldiers were stationed in Australia during the war, and quite a few romances blossomed between servicemen and Australian women. After the war, the Americans brought their Australian brides with them to the United States. According to best estimates, 5,000 to 6,000 Australian women came to the United States.

Though few Americans stayed Down Under after the war, today many Americans are interested in taking up residence in Australia. Australia has become a popular country, partly because of all the attention the country received from the America's Cup yacht race and from movies such as *Crocodile Dundee*.

Some Americans are finding they do not qualify for emigration to Australia. A list of needed skills is kept by the Australian government, and people who can carry those skills with them are considered for eventual citizenship. Australian immigration officials watch closely for anyone who merely thinks the living would be easier Down Under, where there are so many generous welfare programs. People with the training and attitude to help Australia progress are the ones who are given the biggest welcome.

Although immigration patterns now run toward Australia, not toward the United States, the pattern is exactly reversed when it comes to famous Australians. Quite a number of Australians have made international names for themselves in the arts, popular entertainment, sports, politics, publishing, and the sciences. Australia has produced Nobel Prize winners and great stars.

The world-acclaimed opera singer Joan Sutherland is an example of the trend for talented Aussies to leave Australia. Sydney, where her voice was first noticed, is a wonderful place, but the most important center of opera is in Europe, and then in the United States. Before she could be known in the way she is today, she had to move to Europe and sing before the critics and audiences there.

Doctor Helen Caldicott is a respected physician and a specialist in cystic fibrosis, a lung disorder that affects children. But what she is known for internationally is her crusade to rid the world of nuclear weapons. Caldicott traveled from Australia to the United States to practice medicine at Harvard and because she believes that the

Doctor Helen Caldicott

United States can make a difference in the state of worldwide nuclear issues. She gives speeches, writes books, and produces television programs. She produced the film *If You Love This Planet*.

Jill Ker Conway, who was born in Hillston, New South Wales, not far from Sydney, is a distinguished scholar who has also come to the United States. She served as president of Smith College, Northhampton, Mass., from 1975 to 1985.

Australia has many fine authors, one of the most famous being Colleen McCullough. She wrote the international bestseller *The Thorn Birds*. This book, a grim story about life in the Outback, was later made into a made-for-television movie.

Thomas Kenneally wrote the book *Schindler's List*, about a German businessman who saved many Jews from the Holocaust in Europe during World War II. The book was later made into a movie that won an Academy Award.

Perhaps the author who can best teach the outsider about the people and countryside of Australia is Arthur W. Upfield. He wrote mysteries set in the Australian Outback, and his hero is Inspector Napoleon Bonaparte, an Aborigine who was raised from infancy by a European family. Bony, as this unusual policeman is known, understands the bush country and understands human beings. The adventures Upfield gives to him are both thrilling and informative. Many American libraries have Upfield's stories on their shelves.

Some popular musicians leave Australia to make more money. In Australia's population of over 16 million, a rock group could possibly sell enough recordings to make a very good living. But the chance to strike it rich in America's market is much greater.

Several Australian rock groups have become popular in America. Among them are Air Supply, Men at Work, Little River Band, Midnight Oil, and INXS. The Bee Gees were popular in the 1960s and then again in the late 1970s. Singer Helen Reddy is an Australian who made her stage debut at the age of four, when she appeared in Perth in her family's vaudeville act.

A quite special Australian act just getting wider exposure around the world is Yothu Yindi, a rock band. It is made up of Aborigines from the remote Arnhem coast of northern Australia. Yothu Yindi (the words mean mother and child) have appeared in Washington, D.C., at the Kennedy Center.

Australians don't mind when their stars and heroes leave Down Under for greater acclaim and bigger pay. Australians respect talent and ability, and they understand that theirs is not the world's main stage. However, Aussies do expect a degree of loyalty from the stars who leave Australia. In 1977, when the rock group Air Supply went

*The Aborigine Rock Group Yothu Yindi has caught the attention
of American audiences.*

on a tour with Rod Stewart, Australian fans accused the group of abandoning them for glamour elsewhere. So in 1982, on Air Supply's second American tour, the group took along stage props to create a backdrop of an Australian landscape to make the Aussies happy.

Hollywood pays bigger dollars than any other film center in the world, so that is where the best of Australia's movie actors and directors hope to be invited. Sports stars, too, can make more money in the United States if they succeed.

Peter Weir, who directed *Mosquito Coast, Witness, Gallipoli, Picnic at Hanging Rock* and *The Year of Living Dangerously,* is Australian. So is Fred Schepisi, who directed *Plenty, Barbarosa,* and *The Chant of Jimmie Blacksmith.*

Paul Hogan, star and screenwriter of *Crocodile Dundee,* which led all films in America in box-office receipts for a number of weeks in late 1986, is as Australian as they come. He was already famous in the United States for his commercials for Foster's Lager and the Australian Tourist Commission. *Crocodile Dundee,* with its happy-go-lucky hero, its crocodiles, and its kangaroos, has done wonders for Australian tourism.

Mel Gibson, star of the *Mad Max* and *Lethal Weapon* movies, *Forever Young,* and *Braveheart,* can be counted among Australians we have all heard of, although he was

born in America. He moved to Australia when he was young and has lived there for most of his life.

The same is true for singer and actor Olivia Newton-John. She was born in England and moved to Australia when she was five years old. She starred in *Grease* with John Travolta and appeared in the musical fantasy *Xanadu*. Nicole Kidman, who is married to the American actor Tom Cruise, is also an Australian.

Australia has given the world entrepreneurs as well as stars. Rupert Murdoch, whose companies own the Fox Television Network in the United States as well as American newspapers, began building an immense fortune with a newspaper he inherited in Australia. Born in Melbourne, he became a United States citizen in 1985.

Though Australians don't mind losing their national talents to an international arena, they will turn angrily on a star or a hero who gets a big head. Talent, yes; ego, no. Stars and heroes are expected to act like plain folks, without airs, like mates. No one gets dropped more quickly than the star who acts like one.

When an Australian rock star finishes a concert, he or she can walk out through the crowd without being mobbed, without anyone's making a fuss. People might call out, "Nice sounds, Mary," or "Good on ya, mates," but that's it. Once the show is over, the star is just another man or woman.

Paul Hogan, also known as Crocodile Dundee, is a great favorite among Americans.

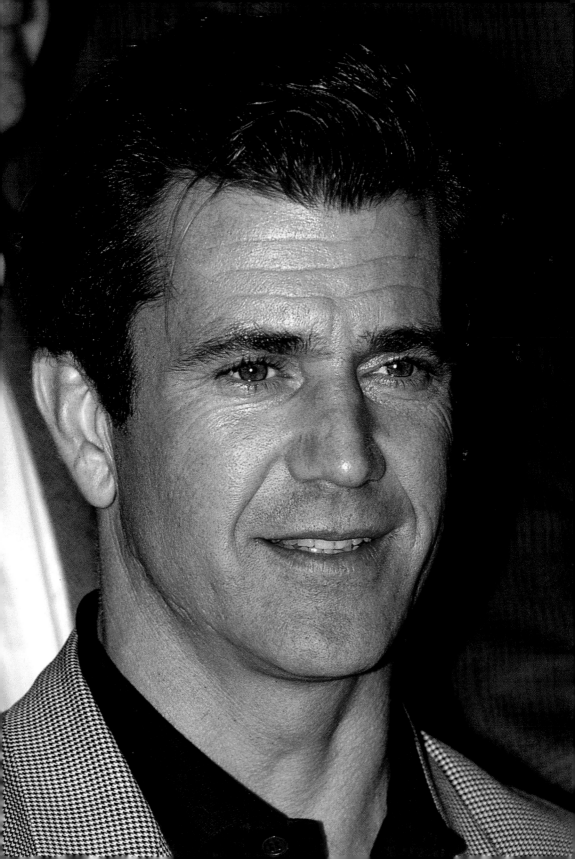

When Joan Sutherland finishes a performance at the Sydney Opera House, fans always wait for her at the stage door. When she emerges, she is not surrounded by bodyguards or by people who specialize in brushing off the fans. She and her husband, the Australian conductor Richard Bonynge, walk out together, without help.

They head right over to the waiting fans, and they chat as if they were old friends. They don't hurry; they stay as long as the fans have something to say. This is very Australian—relaxed, informal, and friendly. Fan and star have different talents, but they meet in a way that says clearly that each person is of value, neither more important than the other. Much of what is special about Australia is captured in a moment like this.

As Americans learn more and more about Australia and its wonderful climate and lifestyle, its appeal grows. Many like the general feeling of well-being in Australia. Australia's cities are bright and clean, and life seems quieter and less stressful than life in the fast-paced American society. But Australia's most appealing qualities come from the people themselves. The warmth and sense of humor of the colorful Aussies are truly what make Australia a lucky land.

Movie star Mel Gibson has lived in Australia most of his life.

Appendix A

Australian Slang

English is the language of Australia, and Australians are capable of speaking it just as properly as it is spoken in the Queen's court of London. But Australia also has a rich slang all its own. Here are some examples.

barby—a barbecue

bikey—a biker

billy—a tin can (or any other container) that is used to boil water for tea over a fire in the bush. A store-bought teakettle on the stove in a modern Australian kitchen is also called a billy.

bloke—a man. We would say fellow or guy.

bludger—a sponger, a moocher, or one who lives off others

bonzer—terrific, as in "That movie is bonzer!" or "She's a bonzer girl!"

bushranger—a bandit or an outlaw

chook—a chicken

cobber—a friend

corroboree   (koh ROB oh ree)—Aborigine festival

Crissie—Christmas

crook—broken or sick, as in "I'm crook. I think it's the flu," or "My car is crook. I think it's the starter."

cuppa—a cup of tea

dero—a derelict

digger—an Australian soldier

dinkum—genuine, or the real thing. A dinkum hero is one whose heroism cannot be doubted or questioned. *Fair dinkum* means "the whole truth."

dunny—an outhouse

flash—showoff, as in "Who's driving that flash car?"

flog—to sell or hock

footie—football

garbo—garbage man

good on ya!—good for you!

grizzle—to complain

joey—a baby kangaroo still in the pouch

knackered—tired

larrikin—a tough guy or hoodlum

mate—a best buddy, a comrade; not a spouse

mossie (or mozzie)—a mosquito

nick—to steal

nit—a fool

ocker—a bumpkin or loudmouth

postie—a postman

roo—a kangaroo

salvo—a member of the Salvation Army

She'll be apples—It will be all right.

silvertail—someone who thinks he or she belongs in high society

slats—ribs

snags—sausages

stickybeak—a busybody

too right!—exactly!

uni—a university

walkabout—to wander. This term comes from the early days when men who tired of a job or a place would put their belongings on their backs and set off on foot. They were said to have gone walkabout.

walloper—a policeman

wowser—a killjoy or party pooper

Appendix B

Consulates and Embassies in the United States and Canada

Australian Consulates in the United States and Canada offer assistance and resource information to Americans and Canadians who want to learn more about Australia.

U.S. Embassy and Consulates

Washington, D. C.
>
> Embassy of Australia
> 1601 Massachusetts Avenue Northwest
> Washington, D.C. 20036
> Phone (202) 797-3000

Honolulu, Hawaii
>
> Consulate General of Australia
> 1000 Bishop Street
> Honolulu, Hawaii 96813
> Phone (808) 524-5050

Houston, Texas
>
> Consulate General of Australia
> 1990 Post Oak Road
> Houston, Texas 77056
> Phone (713) 629-9131

Los Angeles, California
>
> Consulate General of Australia
> 611 North Larchmont Boulevard
> Los Angeles, California 90004
> Phone (213) 469-4300

New York, New York
>
> Consulate General of Australia
> 630 Fifth Avenue, No. 420
> New York, NY 10111
> Phone (212) 408-8400

San Francisco, California
>
> Consulate General of Australia
> 1 Bush Street
> San Francisco, California 95113
> Phone (415) 362-6160

Canadian Embassy and Consulates

Ottawa, Ontario
> Office of the High Commissioner
> 50 O'Connor Street
> Ottawa, Ontario K1P6L2
> Phone (613) 236-0841

Toronto, Ontario
> Consulate General of Australia
> 175 Bloor Street
> Toronto, Ontario M41J3R
> Phone (416) 323-3918

Vancouver, British Columbia
> Consulate General of Australia
> 999 Canada Place
> Vancouver, British Columbia
> V6C3E1
> Phone (604) 644-1177

Australia also maintains a mission at the United Nations and has tourism offices in New York, Los Angeles, and Toronto.

> United Nations
> 1 Dag Hammarskjold Plaza
> New York, New York 10017

SELECTED BIBLIOGRAPHY

Bernardi, Debra, ed. *Fodor's Australia, New Zealand, and the South Pacific*. New York: Fodor's Modern Guides, 1987.

Clifton, T. "The Laid-Back and Lucky Land." *Newsweek* (February 2, 1987):38–39.

Christmas, Linda. *The Ribbon and the Ragged Square: An Australian Journey*. Middlesex: Penguin Books, 1986.

Ellis, Jean A. *From the Dreamtime: Australian Aboriginal Legends*. New York: Harper Collins, 1991.

Ellis, Rennie. *We Live in Australia*. New York: Bookwright Press, 1983.

Fry, Eric, ed. *Rebels and Radicals*. Boston: George Allen & Unwin, 1983.

Garrett, Dan and Warrill Grindrod. *Australia*. Austin, TX: Raintree/Steck-Vaughn, 1990.

Lepthien, Emilie U. *Australia*. Chicago: Children's Press, 1982.

Rajendra, Vijeya. *Australia* (Cultures of the World series). North Bellmore, NY: Marshall Cavendish, 1991.

Shaw, A.G.L., *The Story of Australia*. 5th ed., rev. Boston: Faber & Faber, 1983.

Ward, Russel. *The History of Australia: The Twentieth Century*. New York: Harper & Row, 1977.

INDEX

About the Author

Al Stark lives in Detroit, Michigan, and is the father of six children. He is the author of another book in this series, *Zimbabwe: A Treasure in Africa.*

Stark traveled to Australia for the *Detroit News* in 1986. He wrote a series of articles about the land and the people in advance of the America's Cup yacht races that year. His daughter Allana accompanied him on his trip to Australia and helped him with this book.